HULL CAPT. R. THOMPSON

RIX SHIPPING

Graham Atkinson and John Rix

Ships in Focus Publications

Published in the UK in 2014 by Ships in Focus Publications
18 Franklands, Longton
Preston PR4 5PD

Printed in the UK by Amadeus Press Ltd., Cleckheaton, West Yorkshire

ISBN 978-1-901703-59-7

Front cover:	Jarrix (1) of 1917. *[Company archives]* Lizrix (2) of 2008. *[Company archives]*	Front endpaper:	*Pert* of 1892, painted by Captain P. Thompson. *[Company archives]*
Back cover:	Jemrix. *[Fotoflite incorporating* *Skyfotos 111077]* Rix Cheetah. *[Company archives]*	Back endpaper: Title page:	*Pegrix* (1) of 1921. *[Company archives]* *Robrix* (3) of 1937 on 3rd July 1951. *[World Ship Society Ltd.]*

Introduction

The Victorian era is remembered as one of entrepreneurs, with men creating business empires from humble beginnings through their own hard work. There was plenty of opportunity for people to make their fortune; the Empire presented a huge market with Britain generating a vast amount of exports and requiring commensurate imports. At home industrialisation could not be sustained by the underdeveloped land transport system and the expansion of the major cities needed to be fuelled by cargoes carried in coasters.

The beginnings of the Rix venture could easily be a child's bedtime story. By running away to sea at the age of 11 Robert Rix laid the foundation for one of Yorkshire's largest family-owned companies. It started with him building his first ship on the banks of the River Tees and sailing it himself while his wife stayed at home to bring up their family and keep his creditors at bay. After a seagoing career of over fifty years, Robert came ashore to work in the company's office with his three sons. Each of these contributed individual skills to the success of the venture: Bob was a sea captain like his father, Bert was an engineer, while Herbie was a book keeper. Whether or not they intentionally pursued these careers, it meant that between them they gained experience and knowledge of separate professions which collectively protected the family business from outside influences and pressures.

Following the death of Robert Rix in 1925 his sons were able to keep the company trading during the Depression years of the 1920s and 30s as well the difficult years of the Second World War, the end of which saw the company with just a handful of ships. Fortunately, Rix was one of a small number of British coastal shipping companies which had been converted to using diesel engines rather than the steam engines which were quickly becoming obsolete.

It can only be speculated as to how the original partnership involving the three brothers would have progressed in post-war years had it not been for a family disagreement which led to it being dissolved. What did happen was that the business which carried on under the stewardship of two of the brothers, Bert and Herbie, eventually closed in the early 1960s thanks largely to the effect of death duties. The Rix name was carried on to the present day by their brother Bob, his two sons, Ken and Les, and thereafter by another two generations of the family, John and his son Tim, who are still running the business today.

The last sixty years has been one of steady growth for the present company despite coastal shipping declining in the face of competition from rail and later road transport. Originally a shipping company with a side line in fuel distribution, the present day activities of the Rix Group also include petroleum distribution involving over 75 road tankers, shipbuilding, stevedoring, property development, filling station ownership, marine heavy fuel and gas oil bunkering, mobile home manufacturing and car sales. The company's annual turnover is currently £500,000,000. While the company's ships were originally engaged mainly in coastal tramping and later with regular sailings to the Baltic states, the marine business now involves tank ship and tank barge ownership, supplying fuel oil and gas oil to oceangoing ships and owning workboats for transporting technicians to service offshore windfarms.

There are few people in Hull and the surrounding areas whose lives are not touched by the multi-faceted Rix organisation. Perhaps that is as good a testament as any to the legacy of Robert Rix who started building his business literally with his own hands.

John Rix, Hull   Graham Atkinson, Blyth

February 2014

Contents

Opposite: *Kenrix* (1) of 1924. *[J. and M. Clarkson]*

Robert Rix and Sons

From small beginnings: 1841 to 1914

Robert Rix was the third of five children born into a farming family in Burnham Overy, Norfolk in March 1841. His parents, John and Susan Rix, were farmers and at the age of 10 he was sent to work on the land. He did not take to farm work and within two years had run away to sea, joining a small sailing coaster on the Tees. His early seagoing career involved trading from northern Scottish ports round to South Wales and later the near Continent. With the exception of three trips to the Mediterranean his time was spent on the coast and it was later said that few British ports were unknown to him.

Robert Rix settled in Stockton-on-Tees, where he had joined his first ship, and in 1862 married Margaret Dobson. Their marriage produced eight children, six of whom were born in Stockton-on-Tees: Elizabeth (born 1866), Ada (1870), Barbara Ellen (1873), Laura (1875), John Robert (Bob) (1877) and Ernest Bertie (Bert) (1882). The 1881 Census lists the family living at 27 Skinner Street, and describes Robert as a master lighterman. The family moved to Hull around 1883, and Rix's first ship was transferred to the Hull fishing register that year, and it was here that Herbert Dobson (Herbie) (1886) and Edith (1889) were born.

Robert Rix began in business building small coasting craft on the south bank of the River Tees at Stockton. The site of his yard is not known, or if he even had a yard. Building wooden coastal craft needed little in the way of facilities and it was simply a case of renting a stretch of the shore and laying the keel. Supplies were delivered to the site as required by local businesses, avoiding the need for storage facilities

In 1881 Robert completed a ship for his own account, having been a part owner of at least one of the craft he had previously built. This was traditional practice, the builder taking part of his fee as an investment in the future earnings of the craft.

Robert's first craft was the small, wooden-hulled steamer *R & M*, the initials being those of his and his wife's Christian names, Robert and Margaret. Described as 'a Billy boy with a rudder outside of her', Billy boys were ketch-rigged coasters with high bulwarks, exaggerated sheer and were usually fitted with lee boards. They carried a crew of four, including the master. *R & M* appears in fishing registers for the 1880s and when required could carry about 50 tons of cargo. In order to fish she would need to be heavily rigged to trawl with a heavy net. The net tonnage of *R & M* was just 49 and her trading area was limited by the terms of her

Robert and Margaret Rix. *[Company archives]*

insurance. Her size did not deter Robert and in February 1884 he asked for the vessel's insurance to be extended so that he could trade as far south as Rochester. Three months later in May 1884 the *R & M* arrived in Perth which was outside of his insurance cover. Robert's broker was unaware of this and the ship's mortgagees threatened to repossess the ship as it was uninsured. Robert later arranged cover allowing *R & M* to trade as far north as Dundee. From family records it appears that Margaret Rix played her part in the business even if it was only to keep the creditors at bay until Robert himself was paid.

While never wrecked or involved in a serious incident, Robert witnessed fatalities in his time on the coast, of which two incidents are noted in accounts of his life. In May 1860 he saw eight small craft and their crews lost on Scroby Sand near Caister. In November 1893 he was on a voyage from Boston to Berwick when a northerly gale blew up and he was able to make the Tees before deciding to turn the ship around and run with the storm. In doing so he passed close by *Princess*, which was later wrecked with heavy loss of life, before he made the Humber and anchored in Hawke Roads. Even then he was not safe as the storm carried away the *R & M*'s anchor and cable.

It is not clear why the family moved to Hull in the early 1880s. At that time Hull could claim to be Britain's third port and perhaps Robert saw the opportunity to expand his business. His vessel was principally a fishing craft but would carry general cargo when fishing was slack. Hull was the centre for a large fishing industry, which was why Robert may have decided to move his family and business there.

Robert settled in the Newington area of Hull, on the western limits of the city, close to St. Andrews Dock which was opened in 1883 and given over entirely to the port's fishing industry. The 1888 'Hull Directory' lists Robert as living at 37 Woodcock Street, Newington, describing him as a 'fried fish dealer'. With no business address it is safe to assume that he and his family lived at the back of, or above, the shop. Later directories describe him as a master mariner and the 1892 edition gives his private residence at 20 Marmaduke Street. Later he moved to 9 Devonshire Villas, Wellstead Street where, despite its grand title, the villas housed labourers, fisherman and shunters.

In 1893 Robert ordered a steam ship from Alexander Hall and Co., Aberdeen which was completed as *Edith*, named after Robert's youngest daughter, and was registered at Boston, Lincolnshire. She was mortgaged to

a John Watt. *Edith* was a short raised-quarter deck steamer with a single hold which had moveable wooden bulkheads to subdivide the cargo, and high hatch coamings. The raised quarterdeck and forecastle distinguished coasters of this type from estuary craft. Originally a modest 95 feet overall, *Edith* was lengthened by 18 feet in November 1914. After *Edith* had traded successfully for 18 months, the tiny *R & M* was sold to an Englishman based in France but was soon lost off Beachy Head.

Robert Rix seems to have conformed to the stereotype of the master who was invariably seen on the ship's quarterdeck smoking a long clay pipe, wearing a bowler hat and exercising his shrewd judgement of the weather.

For vessels like *Edith* coal was the major cargo, and at the beginning of the First World War it was estimated that half the coasting fleet was so employed. During 1885 1,300,000 tons were shipped through Hull, the figure rising to 3,500,000 tons by 1904. In 1905 over 4,000 coasting vessels totalling 895,215 tons arrived in Hull, a figure which included both loaded ships and those in ballast. Coal shipments left the Humber for ports anywhere between Bridlington and Torquay. In addition to those loaded locally,

coastwise cargoes available to steamers like *Edith* included coal from the Tees or Tyne to the south coast, from where stone from the Channel Islands or Cornwall might be loaded for the Thames and Medway, with the possibility of a cargo of cement from the Thames for an east coast Scottish port.

Owning *Edith*, Robert evidently prospered and in 1900 he moved to 33 Cholmley Street, a new house in Newington. He was now listed as a ship owner and ship broker and in time his three sons joined the business. John Robert (Bob) was a ship's captain in his own right and Ernest Bertie (Bert) an engineer who eventually became the company's marine superintendent. Herbert Dobson (Herbie) studied at Trinity House School and, because he was good at maths, was taken into the office as book keeper, eventually becoming the company secretary.

During 1902 a larger steamer, *Warrenpoint*, was bought from Irish owners and registered under the ownership of Robert Rix and Sons. Robert continued to operate just two ships until 1907 when he bought *Pert* from the Admiralty which had used her as a dockyard tank vessel since 1896. Continuing as master of *Edith* until 1908, Robert Rix then appointed a Robert Temple and came ashore to operate his three steamers from a new office at 180 High

Robert and Margaret's three sons in their younger days. Left: ship's captain John Robert Rix (known as Bob), 1876-1965. Middle: book keeper and later company secretary Herbert Dobson Rix (Herbie), 1885-1966. Right: engineer, later company superintendent, Ernest Bertie Rix (Bert), 1882-1961. *[Company archives]*

QUEENS DOCK, HULL

Street, Hull. Four other businesses shared this address: two lighter owners, an oil and seed merchant and Thomas Walker and Co., agents for the Boston and Hull Steam Shipping Co. Ltd. For the first two years the Rix business operated without a telephone but a 1906 directory lists the company as having two numbers, one national and one local. The office was near the Old Harbour on the River Hull, which had been the centre of Hull's maritime trade before the construction of the dock system.

Humber Steam Coasters Ltd. was registered on 2nd May 1908 to own the 26-year-old iron steamer *Owain Tudur*. She had been bought from Liverpool owners in April and was transferred to the new company on 20th May 1908. Larger than *Edith*, she was of the size preferred by Robert to serve small wharves and creeks. *Warrenpoint* was lost near the Sunk Light Vessel on 28th May 1908 when she was in collision with the German steamer *Schwalbe*. By the end of the year she had been replaced by a new steamer, again from Alexander Hall and Co., Aberdeen. *Spurnpoint* was a 125-feet, short raised-quarterdeck steamer with one long hatch over a single hold and a derrick at either end of the hatch.

A temporary slump in the shipping industry saw second-hand ship values fall, allowing owners with reserves to acquire tonnage at keen prices. Robert and his sons continued to operate their three steam ships and took advantage of the economic situation by acquiring two more. In July 1912 *Saxon Queen* was bought from London owners and placed under a single-ship company, Saxon Queen Steamship Co. Ltd., managed by Robert Rix and Sons. Setting up single-ship companies limited liability as the sole asset was the ship itself. *Saxon Queen* was transferred to Humber Steam Coasters Ltd. in 1915. In August 1913 Robert bought the 19-year old *Taffy* but her stay in the fleet was brief as she was sold to Irish owners in December 1914. In early 1914 the six-year-old steamer *Ardnagrena* was bought and placed in the ownership of Humber Steam Coasters Ltd. without change of name.

The First World War

The First World War increased freight rates which naturally improved profits for coastal ship owners. A shortage of vessels created a demand for ships, increasing second-hand values enormously so that even older ships commanded sale prices well above their peacetime values. Building merchant ships was not an immediate priority, as it was in the

Second World War. With many yards turned over to warship production, only late in the war did a programme of building cargo ships develop, and even then coasters were neglected.

Saxon Queen was the company's only loss during the First World War, wrecked in October 1916 while on Admiralty service. However, Rix took the opportunity to sell some older steam ships and implemented a building programme to modernise the fleet. In July 1916 *Owain Tudur* was sold to Grimsby owners, although by then orders had been placed with Cochrane and Sons Ltd. of Selby for two pairs of steamers which were delivered between December 1916 and March 1917. Starting with *Magrix* (1) and continuing with *Robrix* (1), *Jarrix* (1), and *Ebbrix* (1), these were the first to be named with the 'rix' prefix. Robert Rix and Sons were the registered owners of *Magrix* (1) and *Ebbrix* (1) with Humber Steam Coasters Ltd. owning *Robrix* (1) and *Jarrix* (1).

Magrix (1) and *Robrix* (1) were 135-feet single-hatch steamers and because of shortages of machinery were fitted with reconditioned engines which had been built in 1900. These ships' ability to trade to remote quays is illustrated by two postcards sent to the office from Palnackie, near Dumfries, on the River Urr, five miles from the Solway Firth. Captain Carter, master of *Robrix* (1), wrote that it would be impossible to get his ship further than Palnackie and even doing this she had grounded for half an hour further downstream between Kippford and Palnackie.

Jarrix (1) and *Ebbrix* (1) were raised-quarterdeck steamers measuring 150 feet with their new 430 IHP engines giving a speed of nine knots. They were to a basic design marketed by the yard based on a hull varying in length from

The harbour at Palnackie. *[Company archives]*

Seen at Antwerp, *Jarrix* (1) was completed at Selby in December 1916 and served the company until 1939. *[Company archives]*

150 to 175 feet. With their bridge amidships for better trim, stability and weight distribution, they were more suited to the Baltic and near-Continental trades than coasting. The ships were more economical because they carried more cargo without the need for a larger crew and also had a greater bunker capacity for longer voyages. The master's and mate's accommodation was amidships between the two holds, under the chartroom and open bridge, with the forward hatch in a well deck. The second hatch and engineers' accommodation were on the raised quarterdeck with crew accommodation in the forecastle. Deck lights were fitted in the forecastle as portholes tended to get broken when coming alongside in rough weather. Rix were among the first owners to fit company bow badges to their ships and in general were regarded as a company which maintained good standards on their ships.

With their growing status as ship owners, Robert Rix and his sons were invited to join the board when Drypool Engineering Co. (Hull) Ltd. was formed in 1916 to acquire the engineering business of Thomas Tate and Co., Hull. The new company supplied winches, boilers and other equipment to shipbuilders. On 23rd November 1920 it was incorporated as Drypool Engineering and Dry Dock Co. Ltd. to combine the business interests of Drypool and the Hull Dry Dock and Ship Repairing Co. Ltd.

Drypool specialised in repairing coasters, barges and lighters with Rix vessels being regular callers for repairs and surveys. However, following the reconditioning of Rowbotham's *Pointsman* (1,174/1934) in 1956 the yard began building ships. In 1965 Drypool acquired the yards of Cochrane and Sons Ltd. at Selby and of Cook, Welton and Gemmell at Beverley. Bob and Herbie Rix were still on Drypool's board when they died and their places were taken

by Ken Rix and R.J. Shepherd, then General Manager, who succeeded Herbie as Chairman of Drypool. Ken's death saw the end of the directorship links with Rix although Drypool continued to dry dock the fleet.

Profits during the war years were good, particularly for ships not on Government service, which earned a lower rate than that commercially available. Naturally, ship prices rose and to take advantage of the situation *Pert* was sold to London owners on 1st June 1917. Although he was in partnership with his sons, Robert had retained personal ownership of *Edith* and he sold her in December 1917, again to a London owner. She was to survive two world wars and was broken up only in 1952 after a 59-year career without change of name.

Post-war recession
A short-lived shipping boom followed the end of the First World War as owners wanted to replace their losses but found new tonnage slow to appear. Second-hand prices remained inflated, resulting in the sales of *Spurnpoint* and *Ardnagrena* in 1919. Rix took delivery of *Hadrix* from John Lewis and Sons Ltd., Aberdeen in February 1919 but less than a year later sold her to Guernsey-based Onesimus Dorey who owned her for the rest of her trading life. A steamer similar in size to *Hadrix* was delivered by Cochranes in April 1920 as *Norrix* (1) but she too had a brief career, sinking after striking the mole at Zeebrugge on 26th March 1921. During 1919 Robert Rix and Sons moved to new offices at Crown Chambers in the Hull street with the wonderful name Land of Green Ginger.

At the time of high freights many speculators ordered new ships and often formed new companies to own them, pushing up the price of a steam coaster by 20% in just

Norrix (1). *[Company archives]*

15 months. But as the boom ended abruptly in May 1920 freight rates fell dramatically and many of the new owners quickly failed. By the time their ships were completed there was little trade for them and they were laid up, some never trading for the owners that had ordered them.

Banks had fuelled the boom by providing mortgages for new ships and they contributed to the ensuing slump by calling in loans and causing companies to default. Some owners survived although making high repayments on ships which could not trade profitably while others were lucky and bought nearly-new tonnage at a fraction of the building price as the banks tried to recover some of their money. Shipbuilders had also provided finance to owners who could not repay their loans, and this plus the reduced demand for ships resulted in several coaster building yards closing.

Economic conditions in the early 1920s remained poor. There were short-lived improvements during 1923 but owners talked of their 'unqualified disappointment'. In 1924 coastwise coal shipments through Hull totalled 297,192 tons compared to 355,563 tons in 1923, both totals being well short of the 932,764 tons for 1913.

Nevertheless, Rix survived the depression and even rebuilt their fleet, taking delivery of six ships between 1920 and 1924, starting with *Norrix* (1) from Cochrane's yard. The other five ships were completed as *Mayrix, Kenrix* (1), *Ernrix, Malrix,* and *Lesrix* (1) and all were to give good service to the company. Again they were named after members of the Rix family except for *Mayrix* which was launched in the month of May and for which there were no family names left to use.

Rix Steamships Ltd. was formed to own *Malrix* and *Lesrix* (1) with Cochranes taking shares in the new company as part payment for the ships. Humber Steam Coasters Ltd. were owners of *Mayrix* and *Ernrix* whilst Robert Rix and Sons, who were the beneficial owners of all the ships, were the registered owners of *Norrix* (1) and *Kenrix* (1). The new ships were joined in the fleet by the second-hand short-raised-quarterdeck steamer *Abus* bought in 1922 and renamed *Norrix* (2) under the ownership of Robert Rix and Sons.

Ten feet longer than the other ships, *Mayrix* carried two sets of twin derricks which proved handy in the Baltic trades and she also had two separate boilers which in theory meant that she did not have to stop for boiler cleaning. But there were hazards to trading to the Baltic: one year she arrived late in the season and was trapped in the ice until the following spring.

Despite the drop in demand for industrial grades, coal remained the major coastal cargo. It was needed for gasworks, for generating electricity, for the steam engines which drove machinery in factories, for railway locomotives,

Three of the company's steamers discharging at Turberville Wharf, Shoreham for the Shoreham Shipping and Coal Co. Ltd. in the late 1920s or early 1930s. This scene was soon to change when Rix lost the contract for shipping coal from the North East to Shoreham. The only ship which can be identified with certainty is the *Lesrix* of 1924 in the centre. *[Company archives]*

traction engines, ships' boilers and for domestic use. Coal from the Northumberland and Durham fields fuelled the large steam fishing fleets based in east coast ports from Lowestoft to Aberdeen. *Kenrix* (1) and her sister ships worked in the east coast coal trade and during the late 1920s *Malrix* and *Lesrix* (1) carried coal from Goole to Shoreham for the Shoreham Shipping and Coal Co. Ltd. In the early 1930s this contract was lost to the Ouse Steamship Co. Ltd. of Goole who put their *Yokefleet* (822/1910) on the run, the customer wishing to make savings by using larger ships at a reduced freight rate.

Rix were fortunate to modernise the fleet but Bob Rix would often remind sons Ken, Les and his grandson John about the dangers of over-expansion. Although there was a modest improvement in trading conditions during the late 1920s it was not sustained into the 1930s and trading conditions did not significantly improve until the Second World War, making it a period of austerity for coastal shipping.

Robert Rix died at his home following a cerebral haemorrhage on the afternoon of Sunday 17th November 1925. Although in his 84th year he was still actively involved in the business, and had been at the company's offices the previous day. He was survived by seven children and his wife Margaret with whom he had celebrated a 60th wedding anniversary in 1922. His funeral at Hull's Northern Cemetery was attended by the Lord Mayor of Hull and representatives of Hull's coastal shipping industry. Company employees included Captain Robert Temple, born in the same village as Robert, and who had been associated with him for nearly 80 years and F. Armstrong who had served as chief engineer with both men. Robert was described as being happiest when hard at work. Into his eighties he continued to drive his motor car, although at a steady 20 miles per hour. His widow Margaret lived on until 24th January 1933. Following Robert's death his sons Bob, Bert,

Robert Rix. *[Company archives]*

and Herbie continued the business, and at this point in the story a digression to provide details concerning their families is useful.

Bert and Herbie each had four children, although Bert's first child died in infancy. Herbie and his wife Fanny had two girls and two boys: Malcolm, Nora, Sheila and Brian. Fanny Rix was keen on amateur theatricals, and her two younger children, Sheila and Brian, took up acting, both making their names in repertory theatre. Under her married name of Mercier, Sheila found fame as Annie Sugden in the television series 'Emmerdale Farm'. Brian Rix is well known for starring in the Whitehall farces and as Director General of MENCAP. He was awarded a CBE in 1977, knighted in 1986 and created a life peer in 1992.

It was through Bob that a third generation of the family became involved in the shipping industry. Bob married Eleanor Londesborough and they had two sons, Robert Kenneth (Ken) (born 6th March 1905) and John Leslie (Les) (born 29th May 1907). Les remained a bachelor and the family line continued through Ken whose marriage to Phyllis Tuton saw the birth on 13th December 1934 of John Robert Rix (John), co-author of this book.

In 1926 Rix controlled ten ships with an average age of seven years, only one of which had been bought second-hand. With a relatively modern fleet, maintenance costs were low putting the company in a good position to ride out poor trading conditions.

Lesrix (1) of 1924 proved to be the last steamship built for Rix. It was 1937 before new ships were ordered again but second-hand tonnage was acquired in the intervening years. This included the five-year-old steamer *Moorside*, bought from Sunderland owners in 1928 and renamed *Pegrix* (1). A regular cargo for her was cattle feed loaded in Hull's Old Harbour for small east coast Scottish ports where she would use her own derricks to discharge.

Malrix fitting out at Selby (top). The hatch coamings on *Malrix* and *Lesrix* (1) were raised a foot higher than normal to increase capacity for lighter-stowing cargoes. On trials *Malrix* achieved 10.5 knots with an almost complete lack of vibration and on her maiden voyage she loaded coal for Bremen under the command of Captain Daly. *[Company archives]*

Mayrix (right) was unique in two respects She was named after the month in which she was launched rather than after a family member, and was the only ship in the fleet fitted with twin derricks at both hatches. *[Company archives]*

Abus was bought in 1922 from Sunderland owners and renamed *Norrix* (2). This photograph shows her under her original owner, D. Hurtley and Sons Ltd., Hull: note the sail. *Norrix* was sold to Whitehaven owners in 1930. *[J. and M. Clarkson collection.]*

Top: *Lesrix* (1) of 1924 was the last steamship built for Rix. *[J. and M. Clarkson]*

Middle: *Magrix* (1) covered in ice at Calais, of all places, in February 1929. *[Company archives]*

Right: *Magrix* (1) aground near Spurn Point around 1930. *[Company archives]*

Robrix (1) was lost on 14th April 1929 when she sank in collision in thick fog with the loss of one crew member. Her name was revived in November 1930 for *Whitgift*, bought the previous month from London owners. *Norrix* (2) left the fleet in 1930 and was another steamer to survive until the 1950s. With these changes the fleet now stood at 10 steamers distributed between three companies as shown in table 1.

Table 1: Ships owned by Rix companies in 1930		
Robert Rix and Sons	**Humber Steam Coasters Ltd.**	**Rix Steamships Ltd.**
Ebbrix 429/1917	*Jarrix* 429/1917	*Lesrix* 703/1924
Kenrix 692/1921	*Mayrix* 794/1920	*Malrix* 703/1923
Magrix 314/1916	*Ernrix* 692/1921	
Pegrix 270/1921		
Robrix 287/1917		

Rix and the Dutch coaster, 1930-1939

During the difficult trading years between the wars the Rix family were amongst many British coastal ship owners who saw the Dutch motor coaster as a particular threat to their livelihood. Bob Rix became involved in this controversy through his membership of the British Coasting and Near Trades Shipowners Federation, which was created in 1924 following an informal meeting of coastal ship owners at the offices of G.T. Gillie and Blair Ltd. in Newcastle. It was formed because coastal ship owners felt overshadowed in shipping industry forums by the liner and deep-sea companies. Coastal owners considered that the Chamber of Shipping was not sympathetic to their cause, as its Policy Committee was made up exclusively of representatives from deep-sea companies. The newly-formed Federation was elected a member of the Chamber of Shipping in 1925 with Bob Rix being particularly active, eventually becoming its Chairman and participating in the debate over Dutch competition.

During the First World War Dutch owners had made healthy profits which were invested in new vessels with improved hulls and machinery. The Dutch had gained experience in inland waterway transportation using sailing craft and many features of these were incorporated into coaster designs, including a shallow draft and a low superstructure so the coaster could pass under bridges on inland waterways. A Dutch coaster could trade as far inland as Kingston-upon-Thames or Norwich, ports which their British steam-driven counterparts often could not reach because of their large superstructures and deep drafts.

The diesel engine was a particularly important factor in the success of Dutch craft. Low-powered internal combustion engines were fitted into sailing craft early in the twentieth century and by 1914 ships were being built with diesel engines. Improvements in diesel engine technology during the First World War meant that the Dutch could now build reliable craft that were essentially motor ships with auxiliary sails. In comparison to steam machinery, a diesel engine meant that more space in the hull was available for cargo, as there was no need for boilers and the adjacent coal bunkers. For the same carrying capacity, a motor coaster was not only smaller than a steamer but, more importantly, had a shallower draft which enabled it to trade to many smaller ports and quays where depth of water was limited.

Dutch yards vigorously marketed their motor ship designs, and their quotations were up to 20% cheaper than those from British yards. They were backed by generous credit facilities so that the owner had to find only 10% of the building cost with the rest provided by a ship-mortgage bank, the shipbuilder or engine builder.

Dutch ships were often owned by their master and were the family home. To pay off the mortgage the master and his family were prepared to work long hours and live prudently. The master or mate often acted as the engineer with a greaser doubling up as a deck hand, and because the oil fuel was simply pumped to the engine there was no need for firemen. Some Dutch ships capable of loading cargoes of 250 tons had a crew of just four. Unlike the owners of British coasters who were limited by the Home Trade rules to working between the Elbe and Brest, Dutch coasters had wider trading limits.

Not surprisingly, Dutch coasters and their owners came in for criticism from their competitors for the size of crew, long hours worked and – in particular – the low freights they accepted. On 23rd March 1936 the 'Times' published an article headed 'Foreign Ships in Coastal Trades'. It reported that in the previous six weeks Poole had handled eight foreign motor ships with cargoes of artificial fertilizers, stone, asphalt, coal and cement, all most likely destined for public works in the vicinity of the port. Southend had handled two foreign coasters with Scottish seed potatoes and Cornish granite. The article found it surprising that so many foreign coasters were carrying agriculture-related cargoes at cheap freight rates when the agricultural industries were 'appealing for the sympathy of the public and financial aid from the state'. An official statement added that 'many complaints had been received of the conveyance of coal for sugar beet factories which are now seeking a renewal of the subsidy' and noted that 'It is remarkable that British taxpayers money should be used to the detriment of a vital arm of our sea services'.

The article drew a response from Sir Alfred Read and Bob Rix, the latter now the Chairman of the British Coasting and Near Trades Shipowners Association. Sir Alfred pointed out that over the last 12 months the number of foreign ships using British ports had risen by 30% and, while flag discrimination and coastal reservation was contrary to British shipping policy, certain countries with no coastal trade of their own were building motor vessels designed for the United Kingdom inter-port trade. He suggested that public utilities, local authorities and private traders should show a voluntary preference for British coasters and that foreign tonnage trading coastwise should be licensed. He finished by saying he had a list of 36 foreign ships of which all but one had been employed by three industries which were seeking or had obtained state aid through tariffs or subsidies. Why, he asked, was public money being spent employing foreign ships and seamen?

Bob's letter, published on 16th April 1936, noted that two weeks previously his motor coaster (presumably the third *Norrix*) with a crew of six fully qualified men on full Maritime Board wages was at Wisbech discharging 300 tons of potatoes. Next to her was a similar-sized Dutch vessel manned by the master, a mate, their two wives and a young boy. Bob had received a complaint from Board of Trade officials that his ship was undermanned and so he asked, if his ship was undermanned, then what of the 'foreigner'?

Above and below: *Pegrix* (1) flying the Rix flag at Aberystwyth, where she was loaded by wheelbarrow. The cargo was probably lead ore. *[Company archives]*
Right: three views of *Pegrix* (1) aground, believed to be in the Humber. *[Conpany archives]*

A sign of the times: the British steam coaster *Knowl Grove* (370/1909) at Littlehampton in 1936 with two motor coasters astern of her: the Dutch *Joma* (372/1931) built at Enkhuizen (centre) and the *Arrivaine* (273/1934) built at Goole for British owners (left). *[J. and M. Clarkson collection]*

Bob, and many like him, felt coastal owners were disadvantaged against rail companies and road hauliers who did not have the outside competition of the Dutch. More trade for British owners meant employment for more seamen and the prospect of orders for more ships from British yards. Bob estimated that there were then 20 foreign ships under construction specifically aimed at the British coastal market. Lately his 'expenses only' rate been undercut by a shilling a ton. He felt it was only a matter of time before the market fell to the 'foreigner's rate' making it unremunerative for the British owner. Few shippers remained who used solely British ships, he complained. He also played the national security card. If war broke out in Europe the threat of air raids would disrupt road and rail links forcing more goods on to sea transport. The development of shallow-draft British coasters would allow the shipping industry to continue to take cargo to small creeks and remote ports.

In December 1936 pressure from the British Coasting and Near Trades Shipowners Federation saw the formation by the Chamber of Shipping of a Fact Finding Committee which, the Chamber's Chairman stated somewhat optimistically, 'would put right anything wrong with the coastal trade'. The Committee's findings were published in June 1938, but did not satisfy the Federation, who disputed the conclusions.

Figures for the late 1930s showed a slight increase in foreign tonnage using British ports. More importantly the actual number of ships increased considerably pointing to the fact that smaller vessels were 'butting in' to the coastal trade. A particular complaint of Federation members was that some deep-sea companies opposed protection of the UK coastal trade because similar steps might be taken by the Indian Government to reserve the lucrative Indian coastal trade for Indian-owned vessels. While the British authorities seemed prepared to do nothing for their coastal ships the Dutch government decreed in 1938 that the Dutch East Indies trade should be confined to ships already employed in the area and when they were replaced it should be by Dutch-flagged vessels.

Although Bob Rix was a fierce critic of the Dutch and their ships, his company became one of the earliest British owners to embrace the diesel engine. In 1936 the six-year-old Dutch-built motor ship *Ellen M* was bought and renamed *Norrix* (3). Buying second-hand was less of a gamble than building a new ship and, with the experience and understanding of motor ships gained with operating *Norrix* (3), Rix decided to order a brand new motor ship which was completed in May 1937 as *Robrix* (3). To free the name her predecessor, *Robrix* (2), was transferred to a new company, Brittain Coasters Ltd. in 1937 and renamed *Norbritt*.

Norrix (3) and *Robrix* (3) both came from the 'Gideon' shipyard in Groningen, in the Netherlands which was owned by J. Koster who has been described as the 'Henry Ford of the motor coaster industry'. Koster's idea was that coaster construction should be standardised and for export, and in both respects he and his yard were successful. In 1932 the yard had completed *Tern* for the General Steam Navigation Co. Ltd., regarded as the prototype for vessels built for British owners at 'Gideon'.

Ellen M on 30th March 1932.

14

Top: The Dutch-built motor coaster *Norrix* (3). Note the turtle-back forecastle, and apparent absence of a funnel. *[Company archives]*

Middle: *Robrix* (3) on trials. Whilst almost new she nearly came to grief. In 1938 a Glasgow company chartered her, primarily to work between Glasgow and the Western Isles. While off Land's End in February 1939 she encountered winds of up to 90 miles per hour when on passage from Hull to Dublin with fish meal. The seas caused considerable damage to the ship and as the storm reached its height her engine began to lose power. Her Chief Engineer, Leslie Stead, realised that the fuel filter needed changing which he did successfully and the ship made for the shelter of Mounts Bay, Cornwall, to ride out the storm. After further repairs she arrived at Dublin the following day. *[Company archives]*

Bottom: Photographed on the Thames, General Steam Navigation Co.'s *Tern* (213/1932) was the the London company's first motor ship, and the forerunner of several motor coasters built for British owners at the 'Gideon' yard of J. Koster at Groningen. Note the similarities to *Norrix* (3) above, including the low wheelhouse, turtle-backed forecastle and canvas dodger. Sold to Cardiff owners in 1949, *Tern* went through eight name changes and was converted into a suction dredger in 1960. She was scuttled in 1989 after suffering heavy weather damage. *[David Whiteside collection]*

Magrix (1) was sold in 1937 to an Aberdeen owner and renamed *Deedon* as seen here and survived for a further 20 years before being sold for demolition in Ireland.

Prior to her sale *Magrix* (1) had an embarrassing experience. She was bound for Hull in ballast with the minimum quantity of bunkers required to get there when she ran into bad weather. Whilst she was struggling into the Humber estuary with her bunkers exhausted the south westerly gale freshened to storm force. Her engine failed because it had no steam so both anchors were dropped but their chains soon parted. The spring tide drove her up the sandy beach inside the curve of Spurn Point and when it receded the ship was high and dry although without hull damage. The next high tide did not

even reach the ship, now settled on the soft sand, and her crew spent the next month digging a channel down to the low water mark. On the next spring tide the ship failed to refloat but by using her engines and two tugs *Magrix* was dragged off the sand and into deeper water. *[World Ship Society Ltd.]*

Above: The launch of *Magrix* (2) at the Gideon yard at Groningen. *[Company archives]*
Below: A view of the *Magrix* (2) on trials supplied to the company by the builders. *[Company archives]*

Robix (3) had single derricks at each end of her 70-feet hold and the only superstructure of note was the enclosed wheelhouse. All her crew were accommodated aft and a stubby funnel replaced the traditional steam smoke stack. With a reduced air draft and hinged funnel and masts, she could pass under rail and road bridges to up-river quays. Demonstrating the advantages of the diesel engine, *Robix* (3) was comparable in dimensions to the 1916-built *Magrix* (1) but could load more cargo on an eight-feet draft. Both new ships were owned by Robert Rix and Sons who also became the owners of *Magrix* (2) built in 1938. In the same year *Pegrix* (2) was completed for Humber Steam Coasters Ltd.

Beginning with *Mayrix*, which was sold to London owners in January 1934, the elderly steamers continued to be disposed of to help finance the motor ships. *Pegrix* (1) went in 1936 and the following year *Magrix* (1) also left Rix ownership. Another change in 1937 saw Robert Rix and Sons moved to Angloco House in George Street, Hull.

Rix in the Second World War
Unlike in the earlier conflict, the British Government took full control of shipping during the Second World War, under the auspices of the Ministry of Shipping and later the Ministry of War Transport. Ports were grouped geographically with each group linked to the Ministry by a Port Officer appointed by the port authority of the major port in that group. The Government's Port Emergency Committee formed local sub-committees to oversee local shipping operations, the Hull Subcommittee being based in the offices of United Towing Co. Ltd.

Coastal ship owners were subject to freight rates controlled by the Ministry through local Coastal and Short Sea Control Committees. There was also a system of licensing voyages to guard against wastage of shipping space. This prioritised cargo movements and facilitated ships being moved quickly to different parts of the coast where necessary.

Short sea liner owners came under the terms of the Liner Requisition (Coasting and Short Sea) Scheme from October 1940. Vessels which had operated on coastal liner services before the war could be directed to where they were most needed with a proportion loading bulk cargoes. This helped reduce the burden on the railways and on road transport which were required to limit their fuel consumption.

Because freight rates had increased prior to the Second World War, the resale value of elderly steam coasters often exceeded their scrap value and in May and June 1939 *Jarrix* (1) and *Ebbrix* (1) were sold to Liverpool owners. The latter sale might not have gone ahead, however, as on 23rd June, just a week before *Ebbrix* (1) was handed over, *Ernrix* sank in Tees Bay after springing a leak.

The two-year-old motor ship *Brixham* was bought late in 1939 as part replacement for the three steamers and she was renamed *Ebbrix* (2) during 1940. She was another Dutch-built ship with a German engine, a notable disadvantage during the war. *Norbritt* was sold in 1940 to a newly-formed partnership which acquired a reputation for buying elderly steamers and working them until they were uneconomic. Government restrictions were introduced

Ebbrix (1) discharging grain at Leith. Sold in 1939, after passing through the hands of various owners with several changes of name she arrived at Troon for breaking up in late 1954. *[Company archives]*

during 1940 which prevented the renaming of ships and changes of ports of registry until the war ended, so *Norbritt* could not be renamed until 1946.

During the Second World War Malcolm, Sheila, Brian and Geoffrey Rix were called up while Les and Ken were not. This rankled with both Bert and Herbie and led to endless arguments in the office with Bob. Bob was semi-retired by now and well over the age for military service. Ken ran the company's ships and those managed for the Ministry of War Transport while Les was in charge of the petroleum business which was overseen by the Petroleum Board.

Les had volunteered for the Royal Navy but was turned down on medical grounds. He had suffered a leg injury when young and often used a wheelchair. Like many people during the war he turned his large garden into a small farm, keeping pigs, poultry, rabbits, and growing a large quantity of potatoes and other vegetables.

In March 1940 the Ministry of Shipping appointed Robert Rix and Sons managers of the Danish steamer *H.H. Petersen*, requisitioned following the German invasion of Denmark, but in January 1941 she struck a mine and sank. Mines had earlier inflicted damage on two other company ships. *Robrix* (3) detonated a mine on 3rd December after her master, Captain Lee, observed a vessel ahead of him cutting across the corner of a known minefield about two miles from Spurn Point Lighthouse. A mine exploded under the vessel and *Robrix* (3) went into the minefield to rescue the crew. She succeeded in getting alongside and taking off the entire crew but herself detonated a mine which caused injuries and serious damage. Fortunately she was able to make Grimsby's Royal Dock but was out of service for some time. *Malrix* became the company's only loss through war causes when she sank with eight of her twelve crew after striking a mine off Southend on 17th December 1940 during a voyage from Hull to London with coal. Mines accounted for another four ships lost in the area on that day.

On 21st August 1941 *Pegrix* (2) sank after colliding with Coast Line's *Normandy Coast* (1,428/1916) off the Norfolk coast. On 8th September *Lesrix* (1) was sold to Comben Longstaff Ltd. under whose ownership she was wrecked on the east coast of Scotland the following January with heavy loss of life. She ran aground in a storm on rocks off Hackley Head and local residents used breeches buoy to rescue four men from the bows before conditions caused the

stern to sink with the loss of ten lives. The large number of casualties was attributed to the coastguard being called out to another ship, *Empire Pilgrim* (2,861/1942), which went ashore north of Aberdeen in a blizzard whilst on her maiden voyage. During 1943 Comben Longstaff bought the 35-year-old *Ardnagrena*. As some compensation for their losses, Robert Rix and Sons became managers of *Empire Ford* for the Ministry of War Transport, completed during September 1941.

During March 1942 coasting owners had their insurance premiums reduced. Vessels qualified for this reduction if they were waiting for or under repair for an aggregate period of seven days or longer over the respective quarter. In June 1942 the Government announced it would pay the whole war risk insurance premiums for non-requisitioned coasting tonnage. Unfortunately, because of the way freight rates were controlled, coasting owners found it difficult to build up financial reserves to meet the costs of new tonnage.

On 10th January 1943 *Empire Ford* went ashore near Seahouses after her engine failed off the Northumberland coast. Her engineer had frequently complained about the engine which was built by a company with little experience in marine engineering. With both anchors dropped and all her cable paid out her engine room flooded and she was abandoned in sinking condition the following day. She refloated only to drift in bad weather before grounding off the Farne Islands. On 27th February she was again refloated and towed into Amble where she lay for a month before being towed to the Tyne for repair, after which she was transferred to the Royal Netherlands Government

For part of the war *Ebbrix* (2) was based at Tenby on secondment to the RAF who used full-sized, radio-controlled aircraft towing a target to train anti-aircraft gunners. At the end of its flight the aircraft ditched in the Severn Estuary and were hoisted aboard *Ebbrix* to be returned to Tenby for collection by the RAF. Aside from these duties, *Ebbrix* (2) supplied the monastery on Caldey Island and on one trip transported a prize bull after which the Abbot invited her master Jim Bore to dine in the monastery's refectory. As the monks had taken a vow of silence the Abbot and Jim communicated in a series of whispers with the silence broken only by a reading from one of the monks. Jim found it a very intriguing, almost medieval experience.

Ebbrix (2) later returned to coastal trading and was fitted with a barrage balloon which gave some protection against air attacks while the ship was at sea and was usually hauled down when entering port. Once, as *Ebbrix* (2) was entering the River Nene bound for Wisbech, Captain Bore asked the pilot if he could leave the balloon aloft. The pilot agreed saying the only obstruction comprised electric cables spanning the river and the balloon should pose no problem as the pylons were 100 feet in height. Unfortunately either the pilot had not allowed for the sag of the cables or the balloon was higher than 100 feet. As the ship approached the cables

Mined in December 1940, the steamer *Malrix* was Rix's only total loss through enemy action. *[J. and M. Clarkson collection]*

The motor coaster *Ebbrix* (2) was bought in 1940. *[Company archives]*

it became apparent that the balloon would touch them. Its upper surface contacted a cable which rode up the balloon's rounded nose making contact with the next electric cable. Both cables were of bare copper and carried 100,000 volts so there was a blue flash, a crack and the hydrogen balloon exploded. The ends of the cables splashed into the River Nene and the remains of the balloon were scattered on the ship's deck. The pilot remarked to Captain Bore that they had just cut off the electricity to half of Lincolnshire.

During the war the company moved offices from the city centre to 103 Princes Avenue to reduce the risk of damage during an air raid. As a further precaution Ken Rix took the company's code books and the only typewriter it owned home with him to Cottingham every night.

In 1943 the Ministry of War Transport gave Rix the management of *Empire Sportsman*, completed at Lowestoft in July. In 1944 *Empire Favourite* and *Empire Fabric*, completed at Goole and Hessle respectively, were also allocated to Rix. The Empire Fs were originally laid down as Chant-type coastal tankers but were altered to dry cargo vessels while under construction.

Ebbrix (2) was taken up for special duties on the east coast of Scotland prior to the Normandy landings and, while her crew were not told the purpose of the training, it was obvious with the number of ships involved that they were preparing for the invasion of Europe. Live ammunition was used and a number of servicemen died during the training. As part of the Normandy landings *Kenrix* (1) and *Ebbrix* (2) both arrived at Juno Beach on 7th June 1944 in convoy EWC1B. They were loaded with petrol in cans which were thrown into cargo nets and discharged over the side into amphibious vehicles. *Ebbrix* (2) spent the next few months carrying petrol between Southampton and the beaches, with fumes

from leaks and spillages lingering throughout the ship. One night after she had anchored to await the tide her crew turned in only to be awoken by the sound of nearby US warships pounding German positions in Caen.

Captain George Simison, master of *Kenrix* (1), was awarded the France and Germany Clasp to his Atlantic Star for his participation in the Normandy landings. In addition to this and the 1939-45 Star he was awarded the MBE in the 1943 Birthday Honours List, presumably for repeated coastal service in the face of German forces. He was one of several Merchant Navy personnel who in March 1944 were awarded the Oak Leaf Emblem or King's Commendation for 'brave conduct when their ships encountered enemy submarines, aircraft, ships or mines'.

After the war Rix managed a former German owned vessel captured by Allied forces in May 1945 and allocated to Britain as war reparations. Renamed *Empire Conlea* her management lasted until 1947 when she was sold to London owners. Rix sold their last steamer, *Kenrix* (1), during November 1945 and at the same time *Norrix* (3) was sold but because restrictions still applied neither was renamed until the following year.

Ship owners who lost ships during the war had the opportunity to either purchase or demise charter government tonnage through the Ship Disposal Scheme. F.T. Everard and Sons Ltd. bought *Empire Favourite* in April 1946 while Rix acquired *Empire Sportsman* for £17,600 in May and after restrictions were lifted renamed her *Norrix* (4). *Empire Fabric* was transferred to Newcastle managers in 1947. Excluding managed vessels the fleet now numbered just four motor vessels, all owned by Robert Rix and Sons: *Robrix* (3) 292/1937, *Ebbrix* (2) 251/1938, *Magrix* (2) 454/1938, and *Norrix* (4) 325/1943.

Last years: 1945-1963

Dry dockings and general repairs were deferred during the war in favour of essential work on war damage and conversions. During the war British motor coasters with German or Dutch engines suffered from a lack of spares but gradually British-built diesel units became available. *Norrix* (4), for example, was fitted with a British-built Lister engine in 1948.

It was widely expected that 1946 would see a repeat of the trading conditions of 1919 followed by a collapse of any post-war boom, but this did not happen as post-war reconstruction was more widespread, proceeded at a slower pace and lasted longer.

At the Annual General Meeting of the Chamber of Shipping's Coasting and Home Trade Tramp Section in December 1945, members voted for continuation of the wartime control of freight rates but decided it should be undertaken by the industry itself rather than by a government ministry. This scheme was implemented in March 1946 with Scheduled Rates covering all coastwise movements around the British Isles. Rates and conditions were fixed by the industry with the exception of government and government-related cargoes which were still controlled by the Ministry of War Transport and later the Ministry of Transport.

This presented an opportunity for owners to press for beneficial changes within the industry. During the war much had been written in the newspapers about the shipping industry, most of which had been sympathetic in tone. It was hoped that licences would be issued first to British ships and then to foreign vessels allowing competition on the same rates and charter conditions and avoiding the undercutting of rates which was prevalent before 1939. A result of the war was increased co-operation within the coasting fraternity and it was felt that collaboration could lead to a co-ordination of internal transport for the benefit of the country.

At the end of the war Malcolm and Geoffrey Rix intimated they would like to join the firm. Geoffrey had originally intended to study agriculture while Malcolm wanted to become a lawyer, but they were called up on the outbreak of war. Their decision to join the firm caused the final disagreement between the three brothers. Bob felt the firm could not support more family members, especially if they did not have any shipping experience, so it was decided that the partnership would be dissolved. Bert and Herbie would continue as equals in a new partnership trading as Robert Rix and Sons while Bob with his sons Ken and Les left to establish J.R. Rix and Sons.

When the partnership was dissolved four ships were owned under the 64th share system. *Magrix* (2) went with Bob to begin the fleet of J.R. Rix and Sons. Bob owned 21 shares in each of *Robrix* (2), *Ebbrix* (2) and *Norrix* (4), and in each case ten shares were sold to Bert and eleven to Herbie. Under the new partnership Malcolm and Geoffrey joined Robert Rix and Sons whilst Bert and Herbie were assisted in the office by the company's chief clerk Stanley Warren and the Shipbroking Department's manager A.S. Ohlsen. Malcolm was a keen radio ham and also ran a radio shop in Hull. Brian and his sister Sheila continued with their stage careers and had no involvement in the shipping business. After the dissolution of the original partnership of Robert Rix and Sons, no new ships were acquired.

The post-war boom lasted until 1955, prolonged by military aid and re-armament. Freight rates remained steady allowing the three remaining ships to trade profitably but as the decade wore on competition from German and Dutch owners increased with the latter once again accused of accepting cargoes at unrealistic rates. Trade then worsened and the late 1950s saw a period of recession together with increased competition from the railways and to a greater extent from road haulage companies, especially in the 1960s as the motorway network developed.

Ebbrix (2) was sold in 1960 and in the early 1960s two mild winters saw a reduced demand for coal and by 1965 freight rates in general had reached their lowest levels for many years. Bert died in January 1961, aged 79, leaving Herbie in charge of the company. There now followed an unfortunate series of events which led to its demise.

Bert and Herbie had consolidated their business interests into one private partnership and not a limited company as, in their opinions, their money was theirs to do what they wanted with and when they died it would pass to their children. In 1950 Bert and Herbie had loaned Brian Rix £450 to set up Rix Theatrical Productions, which shared offices with Robert Rix and Sons in Princes Avenue. Rix Theatrical Productions proved a good investment for the brothers but was considered part of Bert's estate when death duties were calculated.

Coincidently the company's bank, National Westminster, appointed a new manager at the branch where the brothers banked and this official called in the profits from Rix Theatrical Productions to cover Bert's death duties and the losses made by the two ships. The end was swift, for Rix Theatrical Productions ceased trading on 23rd February 1963 while the ships were laid up and sold as soon as possible. *Norrix* (4) went for £14,000 in March 1963 while *Robrix* (3) made £13,000 when sold in June. The offices at 103 Princes Avenue were sold in 1964 and Robert Rix and Sons wound up. Until then Herbie continued as a ship's agent and broker after which he retired. He died in 1965.

Life on board *Norrix* (4) is recalled by Alan Brinklow who joined her in December 1955. 'She was not a good weather ship. I was on her in December 1955 and the weather was a bit hairy. We ran from Sammy William's (Dagenham) Dock in London with, I think, scrap steel for Middlesbrough then on to Blyth to pick up coal for Ipswich. We had to feed ourselves by paying into a kitty every week, not very successful that trip because of the weather. We steered by an old-fashioned compass, with quarter points – there was no 360 degree repeater on that ship. We also worked watch on watch off, which is four hours on, four hours off. That was not very pleasant what with the weather and everything.'
[FotoFlite incorporating Skyfotos]

J.R. Rix and Sons

A fresh start

Bob, Ken and Les Rix began business as J.R. Rix and Sons on 1st January 1947 with a working capital of £7,000 and offices at Bank of England Chambers, 50 Whitefriargate, Hull. The new partnership had just one ship, the *Magrix* (2). Although only nine years old, the motor coaster's engine was soon to need replacing, and this was done during March and April 1949. Unlike other owners who replaced their Dutch or German engines with British machinery, Rix chose a second-hand Deutz engine. New machinery was hard to source and this engine, although older than the ship herself, remained in her until she was scrapped in the 1980s.

Magrix (2) was a regular sight in east coast ports and after re-engining she followed a trading pattern which involved loading scrap in Rotterdam for the Humber or Firth of Forth and returning with coal from the Tyne, Goole or Hull. A minor exception was barley from Hull loaded on 23rd March 1950.

A limited company, Rix Shipping Co. Ltd., was registered on 21st March 1950. The majority of shareholders were business associates of the Rix family and, of nearly 22,000 £1 shares issued, a substantial proportion was held outside the family. This situation continued into the early 1960s when the last shares were bought back bringing Rix Shipping into family ownership.

At their first meeting Rix Shipping's shareholders were told of the intention to acquire the 20-year-old motorship *Roxton* from Middlesbrough owners. Her £23-24,000 cost included £3-4,000 for a new engine which required modification to the seating before it could be installed. This was partially offset by selling her old engine for £750.

Day-to-day management was to be with J.R. Rix and Sons and she entered service on 13th June 1950 as *Kenrix* (2). While in dry dock on 18th April at Victoria Dock, Hull a fire broke out in oil in her bilges but was put out by dock workers before the fire brigade arrived. This was the first of several incidents involving the ship.

The third vessel for the new partnership was a three-year-old ship bought from Swedish owners in 1950 and registered under the ownership of J.R. Rix and Sons as *Jarrix* (2). At the time she appeared to be the right size for coastal work and had a good turn of speed because of her fine lines. Although the name *Jarrix* had been used by Robert Rix and Sons it was felt appropriate because it was the new company's telegraphic address.

A third engine was fitted in *Kenrix* (2) in late 1953 after it was realised that the ship was under performing. The engineer from *Jarrix* was transferred to the ship to put the engine into serviceable condition.

Repairs were necessary following a collision with the Norwegian motor vessel *Havörn* (4,944/1949) on 19th March 1953 whilst *Kenrix* (2) was fogbound outside Dover while on passage from Middlesbrough to Waterford with sulphate of ammonia. At around 20.00 hours *Havörn* fouled her anchor cable causing damage to the hull of *Kenrix* and the loss of her anchor and a length of cable. After temporary repairs *Kenrix* was issued with a seaworthiness certificate and resumed her voyage on 24th March. *Havörn*'s owners admitted liability and settled Rix's claim of £4,700

A further addition was the 16-year-old *Francine* bought from Belgian owners for £34,000 in 1954. During the war she had been taken over by German forces who had sunk her to avoid capture at Bayonne in 1944. She had been salvaged

Kenrix (2) *[Ships in Focus]*

On 20th January 1952 *Magrix* (2) (above) was on a voyage to Shoreham when she went to the aid of the Everard tanker *Acclivity* (below - 389/1931) five miles off Dunstanburgh Castle, Northumberland. *Acclivity* was northbound from Thameshaven for Newburgh with 400 tons of linseed oil when she struck a submerged object shortly after midnight. Her engine room flooded, causing her to list, and her engines shut down. Distress messages were sent to both Cullercoats and Stonehaven radio stations but received no reply. Flares also went unseen but the tanker's crew burned paraffin-soaked mattresses which were spotted by *Magrix* (2). She took off *Acclivity's* crew, although her master, chief officer and a crew member from *Magrix* (2) later went back at around 07.00 hours to attach a tow line in the hope of towing *Acclivity* to the Tyne, but after an hour the line parted and *Acclivity* sank. Her crew was landed at Amble. In 1953 *Magrix* (2) was present at the Spithead Coronation review. *[FotoFlite incorporating Skyfotos/Roy Fenton collection, David Whiteside collection]*

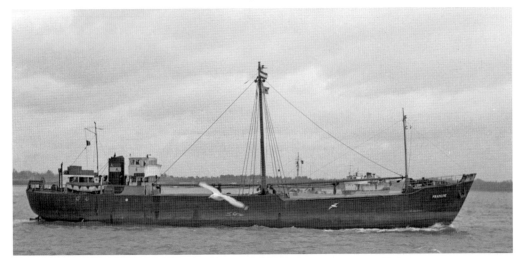

The Belgian *Francine*, seen in the Thames on 9th February 1952, was purchased in 1954 and renamed *Lesrix* (2). Excuse the errant seagull. *[J. and M. Clarkson]*

and returned to her original owners in 1946. After handing over in Antwerp she was dry-docked by Drypool Engineering and Drydock Co. Ltd. where modifications costing a further £3,695 were carried out to comply with Ministry of Transport regulations before she entered service as *Lesrix* (2).

From September 1954 *Kenrix* (2) had been on a time charter trading between London and Antwerp. This was originally to finish at the end of 1955 but was extended until June 1956. Rix Shipping Co. Ltd. had decided to accept any offers for the vessel over £25,000 but on her return to the open market J.R. Rix and Sons as her managers were optimistic about her trading prospects and expected returns as good as her time charter rate.

Jarrix (2) was sold in 1955 to William Robertson of Glasgow. During her Rix career machinery problems had persisted and her new owners soon installed a new engine. By the time of her sale orders for two ships, one each for J.R. Rix and Sons and for Rix Shipping Co. Ltd., had been placed with the Dutch yard that had built *Magrix* (2), *Robrix* (3) and *Pegrix* (2).

Rix Shipping's shareholders wanted further tonnage because they felt their one ship earned too little. They reckoned a new ship with a Crossley engine and a minimum capacity of 700 tons could be built for £82,000 and expected it to load approximately fifty cargoes per annum. Bob and

Ken Rix had the experience and contacts to provide cargoes, J.R. Rix and Sons having regular individual voyage contracts for coal from Amble, Blyth and Goole for Teignmouth, Exmouth, Hayle, Penryn, Falmouth and Penzance. Back cargoes would be china clay from Par or Fowey for the Humber, Sunderland, Scottish ports, Rotterdam, Antwerp or La Pallice. Stone chippings from the Falmouth area or the Channel Islands to the Thames were other options.

New ships, 1957-1967

To help finance two new ships Rix Shipping Co. Ltd. was recapitalised from £25,000 to £45,000 on 2nd January 1957 while on 14th February 1957 J.R. Rix and Sons became a limited company with a share capital of £70,000. Whereas J.R. Rix and Sons had been a partnership between Bob and his two sons, Ken and Les, the new limited company's shareholders included Bob's grandson John with the shares being equally divided between the four family members. Each of the new shareholders made an interest-free loan of £10,000 to the new company.

The new ships were to have Crossley HRN6/350 six-cylinder engines units rated at 560 BHP at 350rpm giving a speed of 10.6 knots. Like the old steamships the motor ships had a single hold divided by a wooden bulkhead and served by two hatches which were covered with hatch boards and tarpaulins. Two three-ton derricks were positioned at either end of the hatches and accommodation was provided for a crew of 10.

Characters from the 1950s: Skipper Syd Bugg (left) on board *Magrix* (2) and Captain A.G. (George) Lee on the forecastle of the *Kenrix* (2) in 1956 (middle). Captain Lee's first ship was the steamer *Kenrix* (1) in 1923 and his last the motor vessel *Bobrix* in 1964. He crossed the bar in May 1990 at the age of 91 years. Note the unguarded machinery. *[Company archives]*

Left to right, in back row, John Rix, Ken Rix and Harold Exon, with Bob Rix sitting.

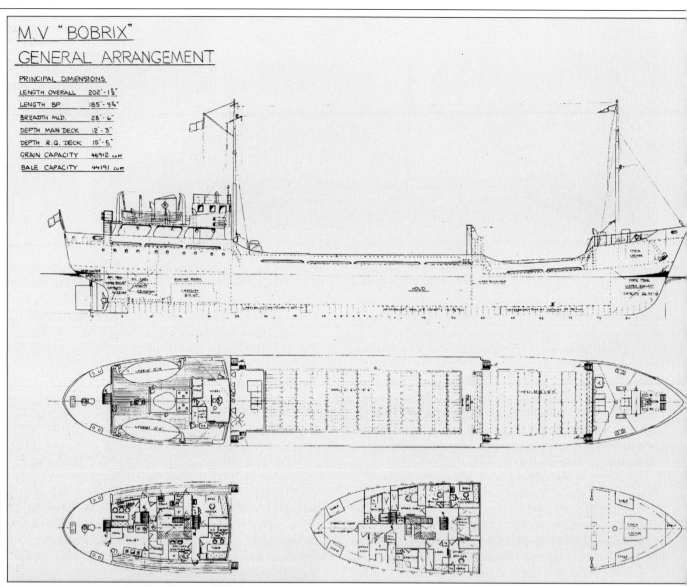

M.V "BOBRIX"

GENERAL ARRANGEMENT

PRINCIPAL DIMENSIONS

LENGTH OVERALL	202'-1½"
LENGTH BP	185'-9¾"
BREADTH MLD.	28'-6"
DEPTH MAIN DECK	12'-3"
DEPTH R.Q. DECK	15'-5"
GRAIN CAPACITY	46912 CUFT
BALE CAPACITY	44191 CUFT

Two new sisters: *Bobrix* and *Jonrix* (1).
Top: General arrangement of the lengthened *Bobrix* and *Jonrix* (1).
Above left: Seen at the keel laying ceremony for *Jonrix* are (left to right) the yard manager of the 'Gideon' shipyard, Bob Shepherd (manager of Drypool Engineering), and John Rix.
Above right: The launching party for *Bobrix* (left to right): Mrs Sellmeyer (wife of the 'Gideon' yard manager), Bob Shepherd, Mr Sellmeyer and John Rix.
Right: *Bobrix* ready for launching with the partially built *Jonrix* astern. *[All: Company archives]*

Top left: *Jonrix* ready for her sideways launch.

Top right: The party on the rostrum awaiting the launch of *Jonrix*: (left to right) Mr Sellmeyer, Don Brown (family friend), Mrs Sellmeyer, Mary Shepherd, Bob Shepherd, and John Rix.

Left: *Jonrix* creates a wave as she slides into the water.

Below: The two sisters in the river at Fowey waiting to load clay. *[All: Company archives]*

The first keel was laid during June 1956 and the ship was launched for J.R. Rix and Sons as *Bobrix* on the morning of 24th November. Originally Phyllis Rix was to carry out the naming ceremony but, because Ken was advised not to travel because of his heart condition, the ship was launched by Mrs Sellmeyer, wife of the yard manager. John represented the family. *Bobrix* took some persuading to enter the water as everything was frozen due to the particularly hard winter. She ran trials on 23th February 1957 and two days later Captain George Simison brought her to Hull to load coke for Rouen.

Sister ship *Jonrix* (1) was launched on 6th April 1957 and delivered on 1st June for £78,470, slightly less than her contract price. Owners were Rix Shipping Co. Ltd. who were prepared to sell the ship before she was handed over if they did not have sufficient funds to pay for her. In fact an offer for the ship had been made in December but was turned down as being too low.

The payment schedule for *Jonrix* illustrates how payments were made during construction. At the time no subsidies or investments grants were available and shipbuilders were only prepared to accept a cash settlement on completion.

A regular cargo for Rix was sulphate of ammonia from the Tyne or Tees to Ipswich or Avonmouth. Because of its corrosive nature, the new ships, and those ordered after them, were not fixed to load this cargo, leaving the older ships like *Kenrix* (2) to do the dirty work, quite literally.

The value of *Kenrix* had been revised to over £20,000 and in December 1957 an offer of £27,000 was received. Handover was scheduled for February 1958 at Hull but the sale fell through when the prospective owners realised the vessel was not suitable for their needs.

Payment schedule for *Jonrix* (1)		
On signing contract	19th January 1956	5%
Six monthly interval	15th May 1956	5%
Keel laid	17th December 1956	15%
Framed	12th February 1957	15%
Plated	20th March 1957	15%
Launch	6th April 1957	20%
Delivery	1st June 1957	25%

New opportunities

In 1958 John discovered that English agricultural limestone was in demand in Scotland. Contacting a friend in the quarry business in North Yorkshire, a trial cargo of 550 tons was loaded on the *Magrix* (2) at Whitby on 1st August 1958 for discharge at Perth. The outcome was encouraging and the ship returned for a second cargo. On behalf of the quarry owner depots were opened by Ken Rix at various eastern Scottish ports. However, the quarry owner then, without consultation with Rix, took a 500-ton Dutch vessel on time charter and the work for Rix ships disappeared overnight.

The Rix family were not known for being backward in such circumstances, so Ken immediately went to Scotland again and arranged for Rix to have its own depots at Kirkcaldy, Dundee, Perth, Montrose and Peterhead. Rix Limes Ltd. was formed and equipped with tipper lorries, loading shovels and lime spreaders. The new company prospered with Scottish sales exceeding 100,000 tons annually, providing regular work for the ships.

Most of the cargoes were loaded at Seaham Harbour but there was a demand for ground chalk and this came by rail to Hull docks from a quarry at Little Weighton in East

Bobrix sails from Whitby with a cargo of limestone. Sheeted down between the holds are self-dumping grabs which operated from the ship's derricks. *[Company archives]*

A Rix lime-spreading wagon. *[Company archives]*

Phyllis Rix, Ken Rix (John Rix's parents) and the manager of the Appingedam shipyard (centre) at the launch of *Kenrix* (3) on 12th September 1959. *[John Rix]*

Yorkshire. During periods of high demand the quarry did not have the manpower to cope so John organised and led a team from the office which worked in the quarry from 18.00 until midnight on a regular basis. Eventually a source of ground chalk was found which meant a ship could be loaded at a berth on the River Trent.

Gains and losses

The optimism of 1956 was countered by poor trading conditions resulting from the 1957 Suez Crisis. The mild winter of 1956/57 caused a drop in levels of coal and grit shipments which were regular winter coastal cargoes. *Jonrix* (1) received preference over *Kenrix* (2) for cargoes as her managers considered her a good earner although they conceded that an offer for *Jonrix* (1) in the region of £80,000 would be acceptable.

Every effort was made to sell *Kenrix* (2) and an offer was received from Greek owners in 1958. This was accepted because prospects for ships of her size and age were poor and her next special survey would require work costing between £7,000 and £10,000. Rix were looking for approximately £27,750 for the ship, a down payment of £14,750 with the balance plus interest over two years. The Greeks offered £15,000 and a cash price of £18,000 'as lies' was eventually agreed. Her new owners obviously took the payment terms literally and returned to Carmelite House with a suitcase containing pounds and US dollars to pay for their acquisition.

Sale of *Kenrix* (2) left Rix with four ships and a replacement was ordered in 1959 from Dutch builders with delivery scheduled for early 1960. Unfortunately 1960 saw the fleet further reduced by two ships, one through sale and one through a casualty.

The new ship was delivered by a shipyard in Appingedam, Holland in February 1960 as *Kenrix* (3). Although 10 feet longer than *Bobrix* and *Jonrix* (1), she had similar tonnage figures and again was a single-hold vessel with two hatches. Her main engine was an unused eight-year-old Crossley engine, bought from the Ministry of Defence and still in its original packaging.

After 13 years' service and a combined total of 22 years in Rix ownership, *Magrix* (2) was sold to Bristol owners in May 1960. After serving a number of Greek owners she was broken up in 1981.

Lesrix (2) sailed from Goole with coal for Hayle on Saturday 29th October 1960 with Captain Simison and nine crew aboard. Captain Simison gave his position on Monday afternoon as 15 miles west of the Isle of Wight and his estimated time of arrival at Hayle was Tuesday afternoon or Wednesday, weather permitting. This was the last heard from her until 'Lloyd's List' of 3rd November reported a lifebuoy from *Lesrix* (2) washed up at Portland. On the morning of 3rd November John Rix had spoken to Captain Guy on *Kenrix*, seven miles west of the Pendeen in a south westerly gale, who agreed that *Lesrix* must be sheltering from the bad weather.

Kenrix (3) takes to the water at Appingedam on 12th September 1959 (left) and the ill-fated *Lesrix* (2) entering Whitby (right). *[Company archives]*

John Rix and June Rix at the launch of *Fylrix* (left) and the *Noorderhaven* passing the Hook of Holland in July 1957 (right). The latter was chartered for a service between the UK and Rotterdam. *[Company archives; J. and M. Clarkson collection]*

An inflatable life raft and two bodies wearing lifejackets were later recovered, identified as the Mate James Owens and Second Engineer Frederick Furness. *Lesrix* (2) was presumed to have sunk during or shortly after 31st October.

The inquiry into her loss was held the following year but could not determine the cause. *Lesrix* (2) had been in a collision on 12th October 1960 and, although water was found in her forepeak while at Aberdeen on 24th October, the inquiry considered this had no bearing on her loss. The inquiry held the ship to be sound and in good repair, and no blame was attached to the owners. Rix had such confidence in her that, because spares for her original Belgian engine were scarce, a new Dutch engine had been ordered and was being built under licence by Drypool.

A near-sister ship to *Jonrix* (1) had been ordered from Appingedam and after completing trials at Delfzijl was delivered in February 1960 as *Kenrix* (3). Rix then contracted to build a sister to replace *Lesrix* (2) which was delivered in May 1962 as *Fylrix*. Outwardly similar in dimensions and appearance, she had a slightly higher deadweight tonnage and

was fitted with a new engine rated at 600 BHP at 320rpm which was built by Drypool and was originally intended for *Lesrix* (2). During her first annual survey in July 1963 she was found to have bottom damage costing between £2,500 and £3,000 to repair. Because Rix ships frequently lay aground, or 'on the hard', the company frequently submitted insurance claims for bottom damage. To minimise time out of service, repairs for such damage were often postponed until a survey was due.

In 1962 Rix joined a venture linking Rotterdam with Hull and Great Yarmouth using the Dutch motor vessel *Noorderhaven* (376/1951). The operating company, Rix Huyser Line Ltd., was formed on 13th July 1962 with partners who were all shipping and forwarding agents: Slavenburg and Huyset N.V. of Rotterdam; Neill and Brown Ltd. of Hull; M. and S. Shipping Ltd. of London; A.W. and E. Limb of Hull. Unfortunately cargoes did not reach the levels expected and the company's first set of accounts showed a net loss of £9,387 for the period from 13th July to 30th November 1962. It was decided that the operation would never become profitable and the company was dissolved.

Management of *Walstream* (485/1949) was handled in the first half of 1964 for her owners, Walford Lines Ltd. She had operated on a liner service and, once this ended, was placed on the spot market with Rix until sold to Greek owners in May 1964. *[Company archives]*

Between the two Rix companies four modern motor ships were owned, all less than five years old and capable of trading to the near-Continent as well as Baltic and Bay of Biscay ports. Seasonal crops were regularly carried, including grain and onions, with French onion sellers and their bicycles in the ship's hold along with the onions. These were loaded at Roscoff in northern France and discharged at Portsmouth or on the Tyne.

Rix Shipping Co. Ltd. came into full family ownership on 1st May 1963 when it became a wholly-owned subsidiary of J.R. Rix and Sons Ltd. which purchased the remaining shares held by individuals and companies. The ownership situation is summarised in the accompanying table.

J.R.Rix and Sons Ltd.	Rix Shipping Co. Ltd.
Bobrix (584/1957)	*Jonrix* (1)(540/1957)
Kenrix (3) (592/1960)	
Fylrix (592/1962)	

The fleet was occasionally supplemented by ships taken on time charter and between 1960 and 1968 these included a number of German vessels loading lime for Scotland, although other cargoes were also carried. John Rix took German shipping students into the office as part of their courses and these were very helpful when the office needed to communicate with the German masters.

On one occasion the German *Hanseat* (379/1950) arrived in Peterhead where one of the last British steam ships, *Briardene* (538/1929), was laid up. The local paper complained about *Hanseat* saying she was a German ship with a cargo for a British owner when a British ship was laid up. It merely highlighted the fact that steam had been superseded by diesel, a fact Rix had realised nearly 30 years earlier.

To the end of May 1962 Rix Shipping's accounts showed a drop in earnings for *Jonrix* (1) due to her special survey which had kept her out of service for 31 days. Her earnings had been better the previous year thanks to a spell in the Baltic timber trade. It was customary in that trade to load the best timber in the hold with the rougher grades stowed on deck so that the financial loss was reduced if the deck cargo was damaged, washed overboard or had to be jettisoned.

Increased running costs combined with static freight rates continued into the 1960s and a combination of bad weather, port congestion and strikes affected operations during 1960. This was compounded by a rise in seamen's wages during September although a 7.5% rise in freights controlled by the Coastwise Schedule was expected to cover the increase. The 1961 AGM reported that *Magrix* (2) had been sold in 1960, and that *Bobrix* had given satisfactory returns thus offsetting a small reduction from the 1959 figures for *Lesrix* (2). The petroleum and agency departments had better trading results as a result of trade improvement in the Yorkshire area.

John Rix negotiated and fixed all the voyages on a daily basis and he needed a detailed knowledge of port costs and other relevant information including bunker requirements and prices - essential if fuel costs were to be kept to a minimum.

The fleet was expanded in February 1964 when Rix acquired the Whitehaven Shipping Co. Ltd. The purchase included substantial tax losses and the motor ship *Whitehaven* which became *Lesrix* (3). In October 1964 *Kenrix* (3) was transferred to Whitehaven ownership.

After her 1965 special survey and annual dry docking, *Jonrix* (1) loaded coal for Teignmouth at Amble which was a positioning cargo for a month's time charter to the University of Birmingham. This project involved mapping the sea bed in Cardigan Bay and was funded by the Royal Society and the Science Research Council. Based in Fishguard *Jonrix* sailed on a Sunday morning and returned on Friday for stores and change of scientific personnel from the University's Geophysics Department. The following year *Kenrix* repeated the charter, which was part of a major survey of the sea floor between Wales and Ireland. The results indicated extensive deposits of oil and natural gas which led to exploration licences being issued by the British and Irish governments.

Rix expanded their Scottish interests by buying the Montrose stevedores J.M. Piggins Ltd. and later renamed the company Piggins and Rix Ltd. As well as acting as stevedores, Piggins were ships' agents and until 1947 had a small fleet of steamers. Montrose had been chosen as the main discharge port for Rix Limes as it was outside the National Dock Labour Scheme and the company had bought a new mobile crane for their own work and other stevedoring. Customers dissatisfied with Scheme ports were attracted to Montrose which handled wood pulp, fertilisers, timber, grain and steel products.

Piggins and Rix (Offshore) Ltd. was created to handle the growing North Sea oil exploration work. It provided stevedoring, agency and bunker fuel services to oil rig supply ships. While offshore activities have been scaled down at the port, Piggins and Rix Ltd. still handle cargo. The Montrose operation now has two large modern cranes, numerous fork lift trucks and expanded warehousing capacity.

When Rix acquired the Whitehaven Shipping Co Ltd. the company came with the motor ship *Whitehaven* which began her Rix career after inspection at Hull's Central Dry Dock. In April she was drydocked at Goole where she was renamed *Lesrix* (3), as seen here. *[Michael Green]*

Minor casualties and charters

In November and December 1965 *Lesrix* (3) and *Fylrix* both suffered bottom damage. On 29th November *Lesrix* (3) grounded after her master decided to take her through the Kyles of Lochalsh while she was on a voyage with barley from Newcastle for Belfast. Some of the barley was discharged into Clyde puffers to lighten the ship which later berthed at Kyle of Lochalsh pier. John wanted the ship issued with a certificate of seaworthiness which would allow her to sail for Belfast where repairs would be carried out. She had arrived on a Saturday and, because the local population strictly observed the Sabbath, there was no Sunday working and no surveyor was prepared to issue a certificate of seaworthiness until the Monday. Consequently she lay alongside; taking more water into her holds which increased her list. To correct her list a further 200 tons of barley was discharged into railway trucks and *Lesrix* (3) sailed for Belfast on 4th December where the remaining cargo was discharged. She was at Harland and Wolff's yard for bottom repairs until 19th January 1966.

Fylrix was leaving Par for Rotterdam on the afternoon tide of 19th December when she grounded on a sandbank. There was a heavy swell running and, although the ship ahead of her cleared the port, *Fylrix* was hit by the swell. Her bow touched bottom and she swung around, grounded and remained fast throughout the night. The German salvage tug *Atlantic* (773/1059) and the Dutch *Utrecht* (638/1956) arrived within hours of her stranding in the hope of being asked to attend her and a buoy was attached to her bow to keep it pointing out to sea. On the morning tide her engine was run but she refused to move and her crew threw some 80 tons of bagged china clay overboard while the Fowey dredger *Lantic Bay* (147/1958) used her grab to discharge a further 50 tons of bulk clay. *Fylrix* started to free herself at the top of the tide, the wire rope to the buoy was cast off and she was able to proceed to Rotterdam. *Kenrix* (3) was in Par at the same time and on 21st December she was able to sail without any trouble for Rotterdam.

Fylrix's hull was inspected during her special survey in May 1966 and a large amount of bottom plating was renewed. The damage was put down to her grounding off Par and she was out of service for a total of 42 days. She later grounded off Shipwash Sands on a ballast trip from the Thames to Seaham but was refloated within half an hour. A seaworthiness certificate was issued until January 1967 which was extended to October when the ship was dry docked.

Several German coasters were taken on time charter by Rix and run by John on the open tramp market alongside Rix-owned vessels. The Germans were all under 600 tonnes carrying capacity whereas the Rix ships carried 800-900 tonnes. The time-chartered vessels were all small enough to transit the Caledonian Canal as their insurance did not permit trading north of Wick. The Canal gave them access to the west coast of the UK.

The first coaster taken on charter was the 500-tonne capacity *Hanseat* (379/1950) in 1965 and she remained on charter for a number of years. Cargoes included coal from the north east ports to Charlestown in Cornwall, with a return cargo of china clay for Reckitt and Colman which was discharged in the Old Harbour at Hull, Rix ships being too large for these facilities. Other German coasters on time charter included *Seebär* (407/1941) and *Gilda* (298/1955).

Industrial disputes

Like all shipowners Rix was affected by the 1966 National Union of Seamen's strike. *Lesrix* (3) arrived from Hartlepool at Holyhead during May 1966 with a cargo of machinery and

Two of the German motor coasters taken on time charter; the *Hanseat* (upper) and *Gilda* (lower). *[Skyfotos incorporating FotoFlite/David Whiteside collection; J. and M. Clarkson collection]*

after completing discharge was strikebound. The striking ratings were paid off leaving on board the master and three officers who were not members of the National Union of Seamen and therefore not on strike. A few days later they were asked to move berth. After casting off she made for sea and John ordered the ship to proceed to Rotterdam for a special survey. This action greatly displeased union officials, particularly as they did not know where the ship had gone, and there was much speculation in the national press concerning her whereabouts. Eventually John arranged with union officials that the ship would continue her special survey work and then remain alongside in Rotterdam until the strike was resolved when new ratings would sign on. John knew full well that it was more than likely that the strike would be over before the survey work was completed and this was exactly what happened.

After the strike had ended one of her first cargoes was china clay from Par to Leith but, while the ship was loading in Cornwall, Rix were informed that dockers in Leith had taken the unofficial decision to black all Rix ships throughout Scotland. On hearing this news John immediately left the office and drove to Scotland, much to the surprise of the leading shop steward who opened his front door that night to find John standing there. The result was that the blacking was lifted enabling Rix ships to trade to Scottish ports without any repercussions.

In addition to this visit to Scotland there were many other union disputes in which, determined to keep the Rix ships running, John was involved. During one seaman's strike John replaced the seamen with Trinity House boys who were on school holiday.

Timrix (1) was discharging at a wharf on the Trent which was outside the National Dock Labour Scheme and John received a telephone call from a Hull docker saying the ship would be blacked at UK ports. John suggested a meeting and the following morning ten Hull dockers arrived at the office. John explained that the discharging port was out of his control and showed them the charter party which gave the receivers of the cargo, Steetley of Worksop, the option to discharge at any Humber or Trent port. John suggested that the dockers should not black his ship but should go to Steetley's office and ask them to consider a Humber port. John further explained that it gave him no pleasure to see ships passing his doorstep to private, up-river wharves as it deprived Rix of agency work. It is not known if the dockers took John's advice to visit Steetley but the *Timrix* (1) was not blacked.

Again during a seaman's strike *Salrix* (1) was kept running between Portsmouth and Jersey after John replaced the deck ratings, told the master to paint out the port of registry, Hull, paint Dublin on the ship's stern and hoist the Irish flag. As the ship was trading coastwise no port authorities wished to sight the ship's papers.

On another occasion he followed a leading shop steward into a local pub one lunchtime and tried, unsuccessfully, to persuade the dockers to lift a ban on a German ship for which Rix were the agents. When faced with a strike on *Kenrix* (3) because of the cook's wage rate he told the local agent in Leith to arrange a lay-up berth for the ship as the entire crew was to be paid off and the ship taken out of service. Threatened with this action the dispute was resolved, but not in favour of the cook.

One dispute he could not settle was a 1979 dustman's strike. *Bobrix* could not put to sea because the bridge staff in Hull would not open Drypool Bridge. Hull City Council had, and still has, a statutory obligation to favour river traffic over road traffic. John offered to open the bridge and although Hull City Council would have allowed this they would not agree that he could close it as this would have been strike breaking. With the bridge in the closed position for road traffic the situation would have been chaotic and could have restricted movements of fire engines and ambulances. *Bobrix* remained landlocked and Hull City Council paid compensation for the time she was delayed. When the bridge master called at Carmelite House later that year for his annual Christmas present John met him but, after an exchange of 'seasonal greetings', he left empty handed and did not call again in future years.

Restrictive practices were also a problem. The first cargo of ground chalk for Rix Limes in Scotland was loaded over the coal hoist in Hull's Alexandra Dock and the coal trimmers turned up even though the cargo, unlike coal, did not require to be trimmed. John went down to the dock and told the trimmers they were not required. Nevertheless they submitted an account which John refused to pay. The same thing happened on the next two occasions after which the trimmers gave up.

Conversions and cargoes, 1967-1974
John Rix considered freight rates and earnings would not justify new ships and in 1967 decided to have the four Dutch-built ships lengthened. Lengthening made them more economical to operate as they could carry more cargo without extra crew. The work was carried out in conjunction with surveys and repairs to minimise down time.

Bobrix and *Jonrix* (1) had their single 115.5-foot hold increased to 130-foot and retained their portable

Timrix (1) could easily have been blacked by Hull dockers following a call at a wharf on the Trent. *[World Ship Society Ltd.]*

31

The first of the four Dutch-built ships to be lengthened was *Kenrix* (3) seen here in March 1975. The work was carried out in the Union Dry Dock, Hull. *[J. and M. Clarkson]*

bulkheads. The single 99-foot hold in *Kenrix* (3) and *Fylrix* was converted to two holds measuring 44 and 76 feet, respectively, with a fixed bulkhead replacing the movable one. All four had their wooden hatch boards and canvas tarpaulins on number one hatch replaced by mechanical steel covers but the now longer number two hatch was still covered by hatch boards and tarpaulins. The canvas covers and beams previously used on number one hatch were kept and used to cover the extra length of number two hatch.

The first ship to be lengthened was *Kenrix* (3), which was also re-engined, the work being done in Hull during July and August 1967. Her Crossley engine was a normally aspirated two-stroke which the makers had said could be supercharged. But supercharging caused many problems and the engine was replaced by a Dutch Brons engine built under licence by Drypool. Her first cargo after lengthening was 826 tons of coal from Goole to Penryn which compared to a figure of 748 tons carried on an earlier voyage.

Fylrix was lengthened at Delfzijl by Scheepsbouw en Reparatiebedrift Gebroeder Sanders. Originally scheduled to arrive by 10th September and be ready by 30th September, she was in dockyard hands from 9th October until 4th November. In January 1968 *Bobrix* had her lengthening combined with her special survey. After she resumed trading on 19th February it was the turn of *Jonrix* (1) for lengthening.

On 28th March 1969 the shareholding in Highseas Ltd. was purchased to take advantage of tax losses, with Ken and John becoming directors. Formed in 1948 as Anglo Dutch Shippers (United Kingdom) Ltd., it had become Highseas Ltd. in 1952. In May 1953 the company took delivery of its only ship, *Wansbeck*, which was not included in the sale to Rix. The main shareholders had been the ship's managers, Anthony and Bainbridge Ltd., and the shipbrokers Harris and Dixon Ltd. who presumably fixed cargoes for the ship. After Rix bought the company *Bobrix* was transferred to Highseas Ltd. to take advantage of its tax situation.

The lengthening operations had been successful and it was decided to treat *Lesrix* (3) similarly. This was carried out at Hull in September 1971 in conjunction with her special and tail shaft surveys. Both hatches were fitted with mechanical covers developed by Hatchway Dynamics Ltd. One of her first cargoes after lengthening was 958 tons of coal from Blyth for the Thames which compared to a capacity of 803 tons before lengthening.

On the afternoon of 1st March 1972 John heard about the availability of *Majo*, a seven-year-old German vessel undergoing her annual survey at Leer in Germany. With Drypool's Bob Triggs he inspected her the following day and agreed a price of DM950,000 (£114,464) when a similar sized new building could have cost approximately £350,000. The sale was completed within a matter of hours and John sat in the master's cabin and wrote the memorandum of agreement for the sale in longhand. He paid the 10% deposit with a personal cheque that was worthless without the relevant documentation. No one in England was aware of the purchase and two days later the pair arrived back home to be greeted by questions from the bank.

After a further dry docking in Hull *Majo* was renamed *Timrix* (1) and became the preferred ship for Rix Limes Ltd. She regularly loaded at Seaham for Montrose, Peterhead, Wick and Dundee while other ports and cargoes included La Pallice (with grain), Antwerp (potash) and Ymuiden (steel). From August 1973 until her sale in January 1975 she was chartered to several companies, one of which was Union Transport Ltd. who eventually purchased her for £300,000 and she was handed over on 18th February 1975. Unfortunately two years later she was lost in the Irish Sea with five of her crew.

Three of the four Dutch-built ships became marine casualties. *Jonrix* (1) was on a voyage from Plymouth to Antwerp with China clay when she sank near the Ruytingen Buoy, ten miles from Dunkirk, at 05.40 on Good Friday, 20th April 1973. Her eight crew together with two children and their mother were rescued by the German motor vessel

Salrix (1) arriving at Preston on 21st September 1974 whilst on charter to Greenore Ferry Services. *[J. and M. Clarkson]*

Nautica (498/1968). One crew member who required hospitalisation was flown to Ramsgate. Her sinking was a mystery as, prior to her loading at Plymouth, she had been drydocked at Penzance.

Two second-hand vessels were bought during 1973 and 1974. The nine year old *Owenro* was inspected at Preston on 23 July 1973 by John along with Bob Triggs. An offer of £111,000 was accepted and the ship was taken over at midday on 7th August and back-chartered to her former owners at £200 per day until February 1974. Built in Holland, she could carry 49 containers and had worked on liner routes in the Irish Sea since her completion, latterly on a service between Preston and Greenore. She was renamed *Salrix* (1).

On 17th December *Salrix* (1) suffered engine trouble and was towed first to Preston and then Liverpool where her machinery was stripped down. She was out of service until the end of March 1974. After her charter was cancelled on 1st January she went on the open market following repairs. When 30 miles south east of Lowestoft on 14th June she was

Involving the family: Sally Rix (second from the right) and friends get involved in painting *Salrix* (2) during the 1970s. Louise Binnington (extreme right) married Tim Rix. *[John Rix]*

disabled with a broken crankshaft and was towed into Hull when she was under repair until August. After a time charter to Cawoods Road Materials Ltd. she was hired by Huelin Renouf Ltd. for trading from Portsmouth to the Channel Islands, a charter which lasted for seven years.

In September 1974 a price of £220,000 was agreed with Hull Gates Shipping Co. Ltd. for the 1965-built *Irishgate* which was handed over at Ijmuiden on 1st October 1974. Her name was changed to *Jemrix* in November. Like *Salrix* (1) her early career was spent in the Irish Sea running with her fleet mate *Northgate* (514/1964) between Garston and Belfast on charter to Irish Sea Ferries Ltd.

When *Irishgate* was bought she was on time charter to the Dutch steel producer Hoogevens, loading at their Ijmuiden steelworks for UK east coast ports, usually Rochester, Whitby or Kings Lynn. She remained on this charter for many years and in mid-1981 was joined for a short time by *Kenrix* (3).

In order to make *Jemrix* more economical a reduction in manning levels was negotiated. By crewing the ship with a master, mate, chief engineer and two able seamen who shared the cooking the cost of a cook was saved. Rix also offered an allowance of £45 per week for cooking which was the weekly budget for eight men meaning the five had a better standard of eating. In 1983 a further agreement was reached whereby the second engineer doubled as an able seamen while the two full-time seamen shared cooking duties.

From January 1974 *Fylrix* was chartered for 12 months by Cawoods Road Materials Ltd. to carry chippings from Dean Quarry, Cornwall, to Belvedere on the River Thames. Berthing at Dean Quarry is a skilful operation that requires considerable expertise. The quarry is south of Falmouth but inside the Manacle Rocks. It is only possible to lie alongside the jetty for a couple of hours on each tide due to the rocks so berthing has to be done accurately and ballast had to be pumped out quickly.

At the correct state of the tide the ship has to proceed inside the Manacle Light Buoy, which warns shipping to stay

Dean Quarry was situated 1.5km from St. Keverne, Cornwall but closed in June 2005 having been worked for roughly one hundred years. Stone from the quarry was mainly used for road construction and surfacing. In its later years Dean Quarry had supplied material for the Channel Tunnel and for coastal defence work in the south east. After closure much of the equipment was removed but the jetty remains.

The top two pictures show *Kenrix* (2) loading at Dean Quarry in the 1950s and that to the right *Bobrix* in the 1960s. The upper photos show the proximity of rocks to the berth and emphasize the navigational skills required. *[Company archives]*

outside of its position, and negotiate the Manacles themselves as well as further rocks in the approach to the jetty. Once abeam to the jetty the ship's speed has to be increased and the bow pointed to a patch of sand on the shore. As the ship passes the jetty a mooring rope is put ashore and, with the bow in the sand, the ship cannot swing onto the rocks; other ropes are then passed ashore. The ship is then manoeuvred astern to the berth where loading begins immediately. Leaving the berth and getting out to sea is an equally skilful manoeuvre as many of the rocks are submerged.

The quarry owners found it difficult to obtain tonnage, especially during the winter when bad weather could prevent loading for several consecutive days. To ensure some continuity they took *Fylrix* and *Bobrix* on time charters and they were later replaced by *Lesrix* (3) and in time *Robrix* (4). While *Robrix* (4) was involved in the trade there was a change of management at Redland, formerly Cawood, and the time charter was replaced by a fixed rate for consecutive voyages. This new arrangement actually proved more profitable than the time charters.

From February 1976 *Fylrix* was on charter to Spedico B.V. of Rotterdam and when this ended she was fixed on a renewable 12-month charter with English China Clay Sales Co. Ltd. In 1983 the charterers became Mineral Shipping and Distribution Ltd., a subsidiary of ECC International Ltd., and

from 1984 charters were renewed six monthly. ECC mainly used *Bobrix* to carry china clay from Par to La Pallice and she was eventually replaced on the charter by *Timrix* (2). By April 1974 only *Lesrix* (3) was involved in general trading and after her special survey in August she began a time charter so that, by the end of the year, all seven ships including the newly purchased *Irishgate* were time chartered. Individually the ships were earning between £280 and £430 per day, which in the prevailing poor market at least covered expenses.

The last years of coastal tramping
Time charters guaranteed work for Rix ships and spelled the end of the individual voyage charters which John Rix had negotiated since 1956 when he assumed control of the ships. Many individual agreements arranged between 1962 and 1975 remain in the company's possession and this is a good point to highlight some of the cargoes, companies and ports mentioned in those agreements.

Records show that in 1964 *Lesrix* (3) discharged bulk copra at Le Havre and in 1965 she was in the Tees loading an ICI ammonia sulphate cargo for Avonmouth. Coal remained a frequent coastal cargo and charterers included S. William Coe and Co. Ltd. and her former owners, Anthony and Bainbridge Ltd. In 1972 she loaded two cargoes of wheat in Antwerp for

Preston on behalf of Mardorf Peach, who eventually built up a sizeable coasting fleet themselves, and in the same year loaded mono ammonium phosphate at Rieme in Belgium for Arklow.

Cargoes for *Bobrix* during 1968 included china clay in Par for Rouen, coal from Goole to Antwerp, wheat from Gateshead to Kings Lynn, and stone at Porthoustock near Falmouth for Ipswich on behalf of the Amalgamated Roadstone Corporation Ltd.

A name that regularly appears in these charters is that of grain traders Tradax International S.A. for whom *Bobrix* was regularly fixed, loading in Rotterdam. Freight rates varied depending on the length of voyage: in 1969 800 tons of wheat loaded at Tilbury for Silloth fetched 33/6d (£1.675p) per ton while 900 tons of French milling wheat for Kirkcaldy paid 50/- (£2.50p) per ton.

Bobrix arriving at Fowey in March, 1977. *[Company archives]*

Several project cargoes appear in the charters, with *Bobrix* carrying a boiler and ancillary equipment from Hartlepool to Chatham for Richardsons Westgarth (Hartlepool) Ltd. In 1970 she loaded a condenser at John Brown's Clydebank yard for Swan Hunter on the Tyne. Irish Sea cargoes for *Bobrix* included gypsum loaded in Dundalk for Glasgow, rock salt from Kilroot for Inverness and flax seed from Antwerp to Drogheda. Coal cargoes were loaded in a variety of ports: Ayr for the Central Electricity Generating Board's power station at Hayle, in Amble for Ipswich and two cargoes from Szczecin to Waterford.

East coast trading saw *Lesrix* (3) loading coiled steel rods manufactured by British Steel at Gunness for Hamburg. Cargoes for *Bobrix* included ammonium nitrate and bagged tetric acid loaded at Immingham and Whitby respectively.

Work in the 1960s for *Fylrix* included bulk and bagged fertilizer from Leith for Lisahally and Belfast, dry road slag discharged in Erith and apple pomace for a Welsh port. She also loaded magnesite at West Hartlepool for Rotterdam, barley at Amble, scrap in Barrow-in-Furness and pitch in Rotterdam for Bayonne. On several occasions she was chartered by Hudig & Veder Chartering N.V. to load garden earth in Rotterdam for St. Malo, later steel coils in Antwerp and bricks in Rotterdam, both for Newport, Monmouthshire. While transhipping is a regular part of coastal work only one such charter agreement appears, for 91 steel pipes transhipped in Antwerp from the Liberian-flag bulk carrier *World Champion* (11,430/1969) for Lowestoft in 1973.

Difficult years: 1975-1984

In 1975 Rix owned six vessels with an average age of 14 years which were split between four companies:

J.R. Rix and Sons Ltd.	Whitehaven Shipping Co. Ltd.	Highseas Ltd.	Rix Shipping Co. Ltd.
Fylrix (1962/592)	*Lesrix* (3) (1957/676)	*Bobrix* (1957/647)	*Salrix* (1) (1965/591)
Jemrix (1965/800)	*Kenrix* (3) (1960/592)		

The yard of the former Humber shipbuilder J.R. Hepworth and Co. (Hull) Ltd. was bought by J.R. Rix and Sons Ltd. during 1977 and a new company, Hepworth Shipyard Ltd., was registered on 7th December 1977 to operate the yard at Paull on the north bank of the Humber estuary. The yard concentrated on building small craft such as trawlers and tugs and in June 1979 won its first export order to supply equipment for a shore-based training school in the Solomon Islands.

From November 1979 until April 1980 *Bobrix* spent 154 days out of service for extensive hull repairs and the fitting of a new German-built main engine. Her new lease of life was to be short. Late on 13th December 1981 off the Channel Islands she reported a serious list to starboard and made for Falmouth with a suspected shifted cargo. The French tanker *Port Renard* (15,979/1961) arrived and stood by. A helicopter from RNAS Culdrose was sent to the scene but *Bobrix's* master indicated that this was not required and the helicopter returned to Culdrose. The situation then quickly worsened and the helicopter returned and took the crew off at 23.30 hours. The following morning *Bobrix* was sighted by the Dutch salvage tug *Noord-Holland* (1965/600) drifting to the south east with her navigation lights still burning. John Rix arranged with the tug's owners, Wijsmuller, to have *Bobrix* towed to a south coast port but shortly after the tug got a line on board *Bobrix* sank after her hatch covers came loose. At the time she was on passage from Bordeaux for Teignmouth with a cargo of maize.

The cancellation of a charter because of a seaman's dispute at the beginning of 1981 meant *Jemrix* was out of service for the first two months of the year and the opportunity was taken to dry dock her to repair bottom and bow damage sustained in 1979. The previous year she had been the subject of 11 individual damage claims by the Medway Yacht Club and yacht owners after she collided with a number of yachts in the Medway on 16th August 1978.

Rix withdrew from the General Council of British Shipping on 1st September 1982 which meant it now negotiated its own agreements with seagoing personnel. One major reason for the resignation was a registration scheme which allowed unemployed seamen to claim benefit while out of work. This was paid as long as they were available to work on any ship owned by a company belonging to the Council.

Kenrix (3) sailing from Eastham on 5th April 1988 as *Deer Sound* (left) and *Fylrix* (right) sunk in Jennycliff Bay in November 1984. She was never completely salvaged. *[J. and M. Clarkson; Company archives]*

When Rix left the scheme two of their five ships were laid up. *Kenrix* (3) was laid up from 14th July until 18th September 1982 when she was chartered to grain traders Bunge and Co. Ltd. until March 1983. She was again laid up from June 1983 until chartered by Orkney-based William Dennison (Shapinsay) Ltd. Dennisons bought her in 1984 as she proved suitable for their Western and Northern Isles trades which included carrying stone for the new Faslane submarine base on the Clyde.

Salrix (1) was laid up at the beginning of 1983 and although reactivated later in the year the company spent £80,000 having her 'tween decks removed by Hepworth's yard. This plus her dry docking and special survey meant she was out of service for three months and did not begin trading again until March 1984.

Jemrix also spent almost half of 1983 laid up. Her special survey was carried out between 17th May and 14th June 1983 and she was then laid up until the beginning of November.

On 21st November *Fylrix* developed a list during severe weather conditions ten miles off the Eddystone Lighthouse. Although she was able to make Plymouth Sound she sank in Jennycliff Bay in the Sound at 03.00 hours on 22nd November. A helicopter from HMS *Engadine* evacuated three of her seven crew and landed them on HMS *Brilliant* while the master, John Ricketts, and remaining crew were rescued by the Plymouth Lifeboat. Her loss reduced the seagoing fleet to three, the lowest figure since the mid-1950s.

Single ship companies, 1984-1994
Shortly before the loss of *Fylrix* in 1984 the purchase of the second-hand *Ellie* had been agreed. She had been built in 1972 at Selby as *Nellie M* and in 1978 was lengthened and had her hatch coamings heightened. While at anchor in Lough Foyle on 7th February 1981 she had been sunk by the Provisional IRA. After being salvaged *Nellie M* was purchased by a scrap company and then spent nearly a year under repair at Londonderry.

The scrap company's operation was a financial disaster. When John and his son Tim Rix inspected *Ellie* in Avonmouth they tried to do a deal on the spot as the scrap man was on board but matters became complicated and the vessel returned to Ireland, pursued by various creditors. Eventually a deal was struck with delivery at Hull, but when the vessel was off the south coast the sellers received the news that she would be arrested on arrival in the UK and they ordered the master to return to Ireland. John had to travel to Dublin and complete the deal in an Irish bank, ensuring that most of the purchase price was paid only when the ship arrived in Hull. The change of ownership enabled the ship to avoid its debts. She was renamed *Timrix* (2), owned by The Timrix Shipping Co. Ltd. which had been created on 1st November 1984.

While arriving at La Pallice in December 1987 *Timrix* had an engine breakdown and was towed to Hull to have her engine replaced with a second-hand unit built for a cancelled contract some years earlier.

Jemrix collided with a Russian vessel six miles north west of Boulogne during January 1985 and required damage repairs in France. While she was out of service *Timrix's* sister ship *Silloth Stag* was bought from Coe Metcalf Ltd. for £303,000. Renamed *Robrix* (4), a time charter with Redlands was arranged for her beginning on 26th April

Ellie, formerly the *Nellie M*, on passage through the English Channel bound for Paull. Note the steelwork on deck fitted to strengthen her hull for the coastwise passage. *[FotoFlite incorporating Skyfotos, 333951]*

1985. On her summer marks she could load 1,120 tons which was reduced to 1,080 tons in winter.

It was decided in 1984 to register the seagoing fleet under the ownership of single-ship companies, all being subsidiaries of J.R. Rix and Sons Ltd. The major advantage was that, should a claim be lodged against a ship, the only asset the company had was the ship itself. A writ would not stop the other ships working because they were owned by separate companies.

Rix Shipping Co. Ltd.	Whitehaven Shipping Co. Ltd.	Highseas Ltd.
Salrix (1) (591/1965)	*Lesrix* (3) (676/1957)	*Jemrix* (800/1965)
Robrix (4) (798/1974)		

Since 1975 *Lesrix* (3) had been continuously employed on Dean Quarry charters and was redelivered to Rix in May 1985 to be replaced by *Robrix* (4). *Lesrix* (3) was then laid up at Paull until sold in April 1986.

Low freight rates meant that ordering new tonnage was not financially viable and to improve her earning power *Jemrix* was lengthened by ten metres in 1985.

In late 1987 a marine casualty was purchased, lengthened and repaired before being put back into service. *The Dutch* had developed a severe list on 27th July 1987 after her deck cargo of timber shifted during a voyage from Archangel to Boston, Lincolnshire. Her engine room and accommodation were flooded and some of the deck cargo jettisoned. She was towed into Hull where she was declared a constructive total loss and sold first to Humber Tugs Ltd. and then to Rix. Lengthened by 13 metres, her carrying capacity increased to 1,850 tons, and she emerged in January 1988 as *Magrix* (3) owned by The Magrix Shipping Co. Ltd.

With the market flat and showing no sign of an upturn, Rix and other coastal operators faced the additional problem of a lack of suitable British crews, especially deck officers. In 1990 *Salrix* (1) and *Jemrix* were transferred to the Bahamas register with *Timrix* (2) following in 1991. The ships kept their British master and chief engineer while the remaining positions were filled by Cape Verde seamen.

During 1987 the Rix group was reorganised in preparation for the retirement of John Snee, a main board director and company secretary who had worked for Rix since 1948. John had been involved in many aspects of the company

Timrix (2) on passage from La Pallice, France to Hull in tow of the tug *Lady Debbie* (369/1978) in early 1988. *[FotoFlite incorporating Skyfotos, 67561]*

Robrix (4), formerly the *Silloth Stag*, was bought in 1985. *[Michael Green]*

The Dutch was bought as a total constructive loss in 1987. After repairs and lengthening she was put into service as *Magrix* (3). She was the last Rix vessel registered at Hull. *[Michael Green]*

as it grew, but particularly the petroleum side of the business. With his retirement due in May 1988 serious thought had to be given to the future structure of the company, especially as it was now involved in a variety of businesses. It was decided that each activity would be managed more-or-less autonomously by a separate subsidiary under a director who was not a member of the main Rix board. As a result, on 1st October 1987 Rix Shipping Co. Ltd. took over responsibility for all shipping activities plus the management and employment of all land-based and seagoing personnel.

Other subsidiary companies responsible for their own activities were Rix Petroleum Ltd. (petroleum distribution), Jordan and Co. (Hull) Ltd. (motor vehicle sales), Hepworth Shipyard Ltd. (shipbuilding) and Piggins and Rix Ltd. (activities at Montrose). This arrangement continues today with the subsequent addition to the group of Maritime Bunkering Ltd. and Victory Leisure Homes Ltd. which manufactures static holiday homes. The group's property portfolio is handled by Tim Rix.

Hepworth Shipyard Ltd. with one of the company's tank barges on the slip. *[Company Archives]*

One of the Piggins Rix warehouses at Montrose. *[Company archives]*

The factory of Victory Leisure Homes Ltd. at Gilberdyke, East Yorkshire. *[Company archives]*

In January 1990 *Robrix* (4) suffered steering problems off Falmouth and was towed into the port by *Jemrix*. In July 1990 as she approached Dean Quarry she hit the Manacles and damaged her propeller, rudder and hull bottom which put her out of action for almost a month.

With no improvement in prospects for short sea owners, on 5th June 1992 *Salrix* (1) was sold to Syrian owners through London brokers for $181,788 and handed over at Rotterdam.

Jemrix was placed on the sales lists during 1994, having continued to be beset with engine problems. Sadly her master Tom Tyrel died on board on 5th October 1994 shortly before she was sold to Panama owners. She was handed over at Ramsgate on 14th October 1994. The day before *Robrix* (4) returned to trade after nearly two months of repairs following an engine breakdown on a voyage from

Rowhedge to Amsterdam. During these repairs she too was transferred to the Bahamas register. This left only *Magrix* (3) on the British register. Later additions to the fleet were also placed on the Bahamas register in the ownership of single ship companies.

Petroleum distribution

Two group companies oversee Rix's petroleum distribution and bunkering operations. Maritime Bunkering Ltd. is responsible for waterborne bunker fuel sales while Rix Petroleum Ltd. covers inland distribution to garage forecourts, road hauliers, farmers, business and domestic heating customers.

Involvement with petroleum began in 1927 when Robert Rix and Sons started importing tractor vaporising oil and lamp oil in barrels from Russia to supply local garages

John Leslie Rix restarted Rix Petroleum after the Second World War and developed it until he retired in the late 1970s. *[Company archives]*

Ken Rix at the naming ceremony of the motor tanker *Oarsman* in Drypool's dry dock in 1958. *[Compamy archives]*

Ken Rix (right) talking to Frank Catton at the Rix filling station at Hutton Cranswick. *[Company archives]*

and farms. Under Les Rix, petroleum distribution was based on a wharf at Ann Watson Street, Hull which was leased from Premier Oil and Cake Mills. Relations between Rix and Premier were not easy. Premier used horse-drawn wagons and Les felt they mistreated their horses which were looked after by the son of Premier's managing director.

During the war the storage depot and all distribution was taken over by the Government. Following the disbanding of the wartime petroleum pool system in 1948, the lease on Ann Watson Street was purchased by J.R. Rix and Sons from Robert Rix and Sons. When the lease was due for renewal Premier offered Rix the freehold for £12,000 as they did not wish to renew the lease. Although Bob Rix considered this price extortionate, he had no option but to pay the asking price to prevent a competitor buying the site.

In post-war years the petroleum business expanded to supply road hauliers and other commercial diesel customers, heating oil for domestic use, tractor oil, diesel and petrol to farmers. The 200 or so customers supplied in the 1950s has now expanded to over 35,000, varying from the former Hull Corporation's City Engineers and Water Departments to small filling stations and independent garages. A fleet of 75 road tankers distributes petroleum products in Yorkshire, Lincolnshire, Tyneside, the Midlands, East Anglia and the east of Scotland. In 2013 17 new road tankers were ordered.

During the 1960s the Jubilee Filling Station on Hull's Holderness Road was bought as an outlet for Rix petrol. By the year 2000, 12 filling stations were owned in Yorkshire, and a car franchise which came with the original filling station was expanded. In 2009 the filling stations were leased to other operators and the car franchises reduced in number.

Rix Petroleum (Scotland) Ltd. was established in 1978 and a small depot opened at Montrose which shared overheads with the Piggins and Rix operation. The business supplies the same type of customers as Rix Petroleum Ltd., and has dramatically expanded.

A pre-Second World War Rix road tanker. [Company archives]

Magrix (3) being bunkered from a Rix Maritime Bunkering road tanker. [Company archives]

Rix sells and delivers a wide range of lubricants in drums and barrels. [Company archives]

The Rix Junction 37 filling station. [Company archives]

Rix Petroleum road tankers under the loading rack at the company's Fountain Road depot. [Company archives]

Rix commercial vehicle service centre. *[Company archives]*

Rix have a fleet of road vehicles for delivering timber products. *[Company archives]*

Jonrix (2) being loaded with storage tanks at Dundee for delivery to Rix installations at Montrose and Hull. *[Company archives]*

On a chance visit to Dundee in 1994 Tim Rix saw that Shell were closing their storage facility in the port and he arranged to buy four 700 cubic metre tanks from the company clearing the site. Three were transferred to Montrose and one to Hull over two voyages by *Jonrix* (2) which received special dispensation to sail with her hatch covers open.

Dating from 2002, Rix Biodiesel marketed biodiesel which it made entirely from renewable sources such as new or used vegetable oils. As one of the largest independent fuel distributors in the UK, Rix had a ready outlet for the new fuel, but the business was discontinued in 2006 once the major oil refineries blended their own biodiesel.

Estuarial barges and bunkering tankers
At the end of 1975 the long-established John Harker Ltd. announced that their tank barge operations on the Humber

would end in March 1976. John Rix arranged to buy three tank barges from Harkers which were sufficient to cover all Rix's requirements for petroleum barging. Rix actually needed only one vessel but three gave coverage for breakdowns, and the spare capacity would allow operations to be expanded.

Beldale H was the first inspected and was bought for £5,000 with *Burtondale H* and *Burdale H* costing slightly more. All three barges remained under Rix ownership until 2006 during which time they were re-engined and had their pumping arrangements and accommodation updated. They worked on the Humber as far down as Immingham under the names *Rix Osprey*, *Rix Falcon* and *Rix Kestrel*.

In 2006 *Rix Osprey* and *Rix Kestrel* were laid up and cannibalised for spare parts, *Rix Kestrel* being broken up in 2008. *Rix Falcon*, which had received a new tank section in 2001, had a new bow and stern fitted during 2006 along with the

Caterpillar engine from *Rix Osprey*. Hepworths did the work and she was renamed *Rix Phoenix* to symbolise her rebirth.

To run the fledgling tank barge business T. and S. Rix Ltd. was formed. Its low start-up costs meant it could be used to involve John's two children in the family business. Tim and Sally Rix were each given 45% shareholdings in T. and S. Rix Ltd. while their parents each retained 5%. Following the death of his wife John acquired her 5% holding. More recently T. and S. Rix Ltd has been fully integrated as a subsidiary of J.R. Rix and Sons Ltd.

Completed by Hepworth in 1990, *Rix Eagle* was the first purpose-built tanker for Rix. She loads 500 tons of products and operates between the refineries at Immingham and depots on the inland waterway system including Rix's own petroleum terminals on the River Hull. The majority of her cargoes are loaded at the Total and Conoco refineries at Killingholme for the Total Butler depot at Castleford and for Bayford's depot at Fleet, on the Aire and Calder Canal. The Castleford depot was opened in 1979 and was supplied by barges before switching to lorries in 1997. Following refurbishment in 2002 this depot reopened for barge traffic and with 12 to 15 shipments each month received approximately 85 million litres of products annually, including domestic heating kerosene, gas oil for agricultural and plant use and low-sulphur diesel for lorries. This traffic has since been discontinued.

To supply heavy bunker oil to vessels on the east coast Maritime Bunkering Ltd. was in the habit of using chartered tonnage. Rix decided to buy a tank vessel of 1,000 tons deadweight for this work, but no suitable bunkering tanker was available. Rix therefore decided to buy and convert to tankers the *Breydon Venture* and *Breydon Enterprise*, standard dry cargo ships built by Yorkshire Dry Dock Co. Ltd. A sister vessel had been successfully converted in 1986.

Breydon Enterprise was converted first. The work was done by Hepworth who gutted her to leave just the bare hull which was divided into 12 tanks for heavy fuel oil and distillate bunkers. The original azimuth propulsion units and her two engines were replaced to increase her power from 760 to 960

BHP, giving a speed of 6.5 knots on one engine and 8.5 with two. During conversion she was renamed *Rix Harrier*. In 1998 *Breydon Venture* was similarly converted and renamed *Rix Hawk*.

Their cargoes are usually loaded at oil storage berths on the south bank of the Humber to bunker vessels in the Humber, on the UK coast or near Continent. Deliveries are also made to UK west coast ports and one delivery for the US Navy was made to Santander.

The tank barge fleet was increased during 1996 with the acquisition of *Artemisium* which was renamed *Rix Merlin* (1). She was exclusively used by Maritime Bunkering Ltd. loaded with gas oil to bunker vessels on the Humber, freeing *Rix Harrier* for longer-distance deliveries.

Another bunkering tanker was added to the Maritime Bunkers Ltd. portfolio in late 1999, the 32-year-old *Eco Supporter*, which was renamed *Rix Condor*, bringing the total of tank vessels to eight.

On 31st January 2003 Veronica Rix officially named a new tank barge *Rix Owl* in Alexandra Dock, Hull. *Rix Owl* had been built at the Hepworth Shipyard for estuarial and canal work as a clean oil barge. It had been expected that a barge with a draft of eight feet could load around 550 tons but *Rix Owl* can carry 600 tons of fuel on the same draft. This is the equivalent of 20 road tankers and it has been calculated she could reduce lorry journeys by 5,000 annually.

At the beginning of 2003 Rix Shipping Co. Ltd. signed an agreement with Waste Oil Service Ltd. of Hull to collect waste engine and lubricating oils from ships in the Humber area for delivery to the Ann Watson Street depot. The waste is usually barged up the River Hull by *Rix Osprey* while that from the south side of the Humber is taken by road tanker to storage tanks in Grimsby Docks where it is loaded into a Rix tank barge. *Rix Condor* transported waste oil between UK and Continental ports while *Rix Hawk* and *Rix Harrier* supplied bunker fuel oil to large ships in the same trading area, including regular voyages to the Tees and Firth of Forth.

The *Rix Phoenix* photographed from Heck Road Bridge on the Aire and Calder Canal. *[Company archives]*

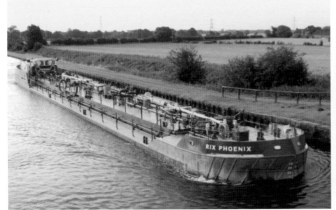

Rix Phoenix approaching and berthed at Bayford's Fleet Storage, Woodlesford on the Aire and Calder. *[Company archives]*

Rix Merlin (1) was withdrawn from service in 2003 and following the removal of all useful equipment was sold for breaking up at New Holland.

Rix Owl operates with two crews seven days a week and is fitted with a hydraulically operated bridge that lowers to clear bridges on inland waterways.

A sea-going tank barge was launched by Hepworth on 17th September 2005 as *Rix Merlin* (2). She began work in early 2006 and was employed in the Humber. Although restricted to voyages within 50 miles of the coast, in theory she could cross the North Sea at its narrowest point on a voyage from the UK to Rotterdam. *Rix Merlin* (2) is double-skinned and her beam is too large for canal work. She is now operating in the Solent.

In 2006 Rix contracted with the ONUR shipyard in Tuzla, Turkey to build two seagoing tankers. They were designed to carry heavy fuel oil and other dirty products but some tanks were to be kept clean for the carriage of gas oil. Double-skinned, they were capable of 12 knots with a capacity of about 2,000 tons. Delivery was scheduled for 2007 and 2008. The cost of each was over £4,000,000 – this should be compared with the £5,000 paid for the first tank craft bought by John Rix in 1976.

The first tanker was launched as *Lizrix* (2) on 17th December 2007. However, because of the delays in her completion, price increases and change in payment methods the second contract was never signed. *Lizrix* (2) was the first ship in Turkey to be launched down rubber bags filled with compressed air. This method is very popular in China and its advantage is that ships can be launched directly into the sea from a beach or quay. Unfortunately as *Lizrix* came to rest she hit another ship which was fitting out causing damge which added to the delays.

Rix Harrier, formerly *Breydon Enterprise,* after conversion. *[FotoFlite incorporating Skyfotos, 337065]*

John and Veronica Rix at the naming ceremony for *Rix Owl. [Company archives]*

The building was supervised by a Danish consulting company, Erria (Consulting) A/S, but after further delays Rix sent two of their own staff to oversee the ship's completion. Because the contract was set at a fixed price Rix suspected the builders were delaying delivery because of increased costs and hoping that Rix walked away from the contract so that the ship could be sold at a higher price. *Lizrix* (2) left the yard incomplete in May 2008, sailing direct to the Humber where she was prepared for service and was named by Tim Rix's daughter, Elizabeth (Lizzie) on 5th August 2008. *Lizrix* (2) quadrupled the company's capacity and allowed them to bunker ships anywhere around the UK or near Continent.

At the same time as the contract for *Lizrix* an agreement was made with an Indian shipyard for two smaller tankers for delivery in 2009 as *Jonrix* (3) and *Timrix* (4), but because of delays these contracts were cancelled early in 2010.

During 2008 both *Rix Hawk* and *Rix Harrier* were further modified

Rix Condor, photographed on 16th March 2007, was completed in Germany in 1967. With the company from 1999 to 2008 she was initially used for bunkering and later carrying waste oil to and from the continent.   *[Michael Green]*

Rix Merlin (2) docking at Hull. *[Company archives]*

The positions list for 19th April 2005 illustrating the activities of the tanker fleet.	
Rix Owl	Loading 500 tons of petroleum products at Immingham for Castleford.
Rix Eagle	On passage from Immingham to Ferrybridge with 450 tons of lubricating base oil.
Rix Kestrel	At Immingham loading 400 tons petroleum products for the Rix depot at Fountain Road on the River Hull.
Rix Osprey	On passage to Drax Power Station from Immingham with 400 tons of oil.
Rix Falcon	Making various deliveries of gas oil bunkers to vessels in the Humber area.
Rix Hawk	Loaded with 950 tons of black bunker oil for delivery in the Humber.
Rix Harrier	Loading 100 tons of gas oil bunkers for delivery to a vessel 12 miles off the Humber
Rix Condor	In ballast from the Tees to Immingham to load 750 tons of black oil bunkers for delivery to a vessel at Redcar.
Rix Merlin (2)	Coastal tank barge under construction at the Hepworth Shipyard, Paull.

Tim Rix and daughter Lizzie at the naming ceremony of *Lizrix* (2). *[Company archives]*

44

with side sponsors to become wholly double hulled. The work on *Rix Hawk* was carried out at Penzance between August and October before she took up a charter with World Fuel Services Ltd. to bunkering ships in Falmouth Bay. *Rix Harrier* underwent similar work at Hull but had her capacity split evenly so she can carry clean and fuel oils on behalf of Maritime Fuel on the Humber and the east coast in conjunction with *Rix Merlin* (2).

Rix Condor was sold to Nigerian owners in March 2008 but, with half of the sale price paid, her new owners had still not made delivery arrangements for the vessel by the end of the year so she did not leave the Humber until early 2009.

After being stripped of all useful equipment, including her engine and boiler, *Rix Osprey* was purchased by a Goole boat builder who offered her for sale with conversion to a house boat while *Rix Kestrel* was broken up locally in 2008.

The last to remain in service of the three Harker boats which started the company's involvement in oil transportation, *Rix Phoenix* was delivered to Aveco Ltd., Middlesbrough in September 2009 to be 'encapsulated', with a new skin built around her cargo tanks, converting her into a double-hulled tanker. Converted to satisfy the requirements of oil companies, she was towed back from the Tees to the Humber to resume work in mid-January 2010. *Rix Owl* was then towed to the Tees and arrived there on 3rd March to be double-skinned.

A chance conversation between Tim Rix and one of his brokers resulted in the charter of *Rix Hawk* by the Romanian state oil company OMV for two years with the vessel based

Rix Phoenix at Middlesbrough on 22nd September 2009 awaiting encapsulation. [Michael Green]

in Constanta. It was originally planned to change her crew and registry at Gibraltar while en route to the Black Sea. However, her cargo tanks were used to provide extra fuel capacity and drinking water was carried in drums on deck, allowing her to sail non-stop from Hull to Constanta. The charter lasted for just one year, the charterers paying very substantial compensation for her early redelivery.

During 2011 *Lizrix* (2) was based in Falmouth, chartered to deliver bunkers to ocean-going vessels, whilst *Rix Eagle* was running clean products from Immingham to the Rix depot at Fountain Road, Hull. *Rix Hawk, Rix Harrier, Rix Owl* and *Rix Phoenix* undertook bunkering work on the Humber and at other UK ports. *Rix Merlin* (2) was carrying clean products on the Solent. The tanker *Lerrix* (2) joined the fleet in May 2012 on naming by Lucinda Emily Rix.

Rix Hawk bound for Constanta, note the containers of drinking water on deck. [Fotoflite incorporating Skyfotos 351965]

Members of the family at the naming ceremony of the motor tanker *Lerrix* (2) (above left) in William Wright Dock, Hull. Left to right (with their relationship to John): John Rix, Veronica (wife), Harry (grandson), Lucinda (daughter), Robbie (grandson), Sally (daughter), Tim (son), Lizzie (grand daughter), Louise (daughter-in-law). After the naming ceremony John, accompanied by his wife Veronica, presented a memento of the occasion to their daughter Lucinda (above right). *[Both: Company archives]*

Tanker *Lerrix* (2) preparing to sail from Alexandra Dock, Hull on 10th November 2012. *[Roy Cressey]*

The Baltic fleet, 1994-2012

The collapse of the Soviet Union and the expansion of trade to the Baltic states of Estonia, Lithuania and Latvia presented an opportunity to develop a service to and from these countries employing Rix ships. Agreements were made, particularly in Riga, Tallinn and Klaipeda, and facilities were made available by Associated British Ports in Hull and at Ipswich. Because the turnarounds at Ipswich were disappointing it was decided to concentrate on Hull's Alexandra Dock where two berths, in-house stevedoring and 34 acres of open land with two large transit sheds were used. Rix had 29 fork lift trucks on site and two large mobile cranes, one of which had a lifting capacity of 200 tons.

Outward cargo loaded for the Baltic usually comprised a mix of second-hand mobile homes, vans, trucks, plant and cars, while the main inward cargo was timber for east coast ports. The ships were fitted with reefer points to carry refrigerated containers.

Timber in, vehicles out. *Timrix (3)* (above) has almost completed discharge of her inward cargo of timber at Alexandra Dock on 10th July 1999 whilst *Lerrix* (1) (below) a member of the Baltic fleet from 1998 to 2010, finishes loading her export cargo of second-hand vehicles. *[Michael Green, Company archives]*

Ronrix seen above on 12th April 2006, and her sister-ship *Salrix* (2), were the last two ships of the Baltic fleet. Both were disposed of in March 2012. *[Michael Green]*

The service began in 1994 using a single box-hold vessel bought from German owners and renamed *Jonrix* (2) in the ownership of a single ship company of the same name. She was one of 17 similar vessels built in the late 1970s for the German Fastbox pool and which proved to be popular with charterers. In 1995 she was time chartered by Humber Marine Services Ltd. operating under the name Humber Baltic Line and running mainly to Lithuania. Cargo levels did not live up to expectations and on completion of the time charter the vessel was returned to Rix who took over the service and, under the trading name Rix Baltic Line, expanded it to other Baltic ports, in particular Riga, Tallinn and Klaipeda.

When not required on this service *Jonrix* (2) carried a variety of cargoes, including the storage tanks from Dundee to Montrose and Hull mentioned previously. Another notable cargo was nine 113-tonne coils of three-metre diameter steel cables for mooring oil rigs and platforms which were manufactured in Doncaster and shipped from Goole to the Tyne. Because of her high cubic capacity, *Jonrix* was ideal for light-stowing cargoes and spent some time carrying feedstuffs from the Continent to various British ports

Late in 1995 both *Robrix* (4) and *Timrix* (2) were sold to a London management company and handed over in January 1996. On 13th December 1995 whilst these sales were being agreed the 18-year-old *Yorksee* (renamed *Lizrix* (1)) was purchased at auction in Rotterdam after her owners were declared bankrupt. She was bought for tramping in the short-sea bulk cargo market and Rix ran her with timber from Riga to east coast ports in conjunction with their Klaipeda business.

Having outgrown the premises in Posterngate, J.R. Rix and Sons Ltd. moved to its current head office at Witham House, Spyvee Street, Hull during 1996. At first all group companies were located there but with the expansion of

The position list for 19 April 2005 illustrating the activities of the seagoing ships.

Robrix (4)	At Rotterdam, loading 2,500 tons of feedstuff for Ipswich.
Ronrix (1)	Discharging general cargo and reloading a part cargo of timber and wood pulp at Klaipeda. To complete at Riga for discharge at Hull.
Salrix (2)	On passage from Hull to Klaipeda with general cargo.
Jonrix (2)	At Hull awaiting a berth to discharge 2,000 tons of hypomeal.
Harrix (1)	On passage from Tallinn to Hull with containers and 2,200 cubic metres of timber.
Lerrix (1)	On passage Hull to Tallinn with general cargo.

the Baltic trade Rix Shipping Co. Ltd. eventually moved to offices in Alexandra Dock.

The volume of Baltic trade eventually expanded to the extent that it could sustain more frequent sailings. Weekly sailings were scheduled to and from Tallinn, Riga and Klaipeda with Hull as the main British port. In December 1997 two sisters of *Jonrix* (2) were purchased. Taken over at Hull during January 1998 they were renamed *Harrix* and *Lerrix* (1). Another sister ship was purchased and renamed *Timrix* (3). All these ships came from an Austrian management company acting on behalf of the ship's German owners.

The Rix fleet remained unchanged until February 2002 when *Lizrix* (1) was sold to Malta flag operators and shortly afterwards two more Fastbox ships were added to the fleet. These differed from the earlier purchases as they had been lengthened by 16.80 metres before completion. They are distinguishable by their extra accommodation deck.

Trading to the Baltic was not so comfortable for those on board as these photos taken of *Jonrix* (2) in late 2002 and early 2003 show. The accumulations of ice had to be removed frequently but there was always time for a joke. *[Company archives]*

Trading in these conditions can cause damage to the hull, but of particular concern is damage to the propeller or rudder. *[Company archives]*

On 4th April 2002 a new Salrix Shipping Co. Ltd. was registered to own *Salrix* (2) and The Ronrix Shipping Co. Ltd. to own *Ronrix* with both ships registered at Hull. By the end of the year their four near-sisters had been transferred from the Bahamas register to the British flag which offered significant advantages. Relaxed labour rules have allowed foreign officers and ratings to be employed on the seagoing fleet and on some of the tank barges.

Rix was always willing to consider suitable second-hand tonnage if it became available and during March 2004 a ship was bought from Dutch owners, although she had been owned by an Austrian company for much of her career. Renamed *Robrix* (5), her spell under Rix ownership was brief as she went to Israeli owners in November 2005 when the Rix company was made a very favourable offer.

In July 2003 both *Timrix* (3) and *Jonrix* (2) were advertised in sales lists and at the end of 2004 *Timrix* (3) was sold to Turkish owners, and in 2007 *Jonrix* (2) went to British owners.

In 2008 Rix operated a fleet of four dry cargo ships with a total carrying capacity of some 12,000 tons which, when not employed between the United Kingdom and the Baltic, were engaged on individual voyage charters. With the economic downturn in 2008 the ships experienced difficult trading conditions. While the end of the calendar year is traditionally a slack time for cargo availability, at the end of 2008 deep-sea rates were as low as one tenth of their normal levels with too many ships available for the cargo offering. Due to lack of demand for timber, mainly in the building and do-it-yourself trades, cargo levels dropped dramatically so that only one ship was required for the Baltic service. Perversely, however, with competitors reducing capacity, Rix were able to employ both *Harrix* and *Lerrix* (1) for a short time on their own sailings. *Salrix* (2) and *Ronrix* were employed importing fertilizers and biomass from the Baltic

states. All four ships continued to load the usual general cargoes in Hull for export to the Baltic states.

In December 2008 both *Harrix* and *Lerrix* (1) were laid up at Hull, although *Lerrix* was put back into trade in September 2009 to start a timber service from Sweden and the Baltic States to Hull and Great Yarmouth. *Ronrix* and *Salrix* (2) were similarly employed and all three carried general cargo from Hull to the Baltic States or Poland. However, in March 2010 both *Harrix* and *Lerrix* (1) were sold to foreign owners.

At the beginning of 2012 only two dry cargo ships remained in service, *Salrix* (2) and *Ronrix*. These were trading profitably mainly because their age meant depreciation was small. To build new vessels was out of the question because their cost would have resulted in a negative return on the investment. Even acquiring modern, second-hand vessels would have been a bad investment. An opportunity arose to sell *Salrix* (2) and *Ronrix* and they were handed over to Turkish owners in April 2012.

At about this time it was decided to invest in wind farm service vessels, 21-metre aluminium catamarans with twin engines of 850/1,300 HP giving a service speed of 25 to 30 knots with a bow thruster for extra manoevrability. The vessels were built on spec as it was considered that there would be a demand due to the national policy of building offshore wind turbines. The first vessel, *Rix Panther*, was built at Blyth and entered service in July 2012, and was followed by *Rix Tiger* in 2013 and by the *Rix Cheetah* from the Hepworth yard.

It was also decided that Rix would retain the ownership of the Hepworth Shipyard Ltd., but that the workforce would be employed by Dunston Shipbuilders, and that Rix would order workboats from the yard. Further vessels will be built by Blyth and at Paull if the initial three are successful.

Tim Rix at the company's 25-acre timber storage facility near to King George Dock, Hull. *[Company archives]*

Veronica and Lucinda Rix with the uncompleted hull of an aluminium work boat under construction by Dunston Shipbuilders at Hepworth Shipyard, Paull. The aluminium hull is built over a mild steel jig. *[Company archives]*

Rix today

A large and diverse company, J.R. Rix and Sons Ltd. is amongst the top 100 private limited companies in the United Kingdom. The parent company for Rix Shipping Co. Ltd., Rix Petroleum Ltd., Rix Sea Shuttle Ltd., Hepworth Shipyard Ltd., Piggins and Rix Ltd., Victory Leisure Homes Ltd. and Maritime Bunkering Ltd., it also owns Rix Trucks Ltd., Jubilee Leasing Ltd., Carmelite Leasing Ltd., Rix Heating Ltd., Maritime Brokers Ltd. and Rix Motors Ltd. which are currently non-trading companies. As well as a 25-acre site in Hull accommodating a variety of tenants, Rix owns a 25-acre site near to the entrance of King George Dock.

The Rix family have over a century's experience in shipping and ship owning and combine the values of a traditional family business with an attitude focused on meeting the demands of the modern market place. The company is still locally based. Its fleet has always been modest in size but because the company remains in family control it is not answerable to outside shareholders, allowing it to quickly take advantage of opportunities when and where they arise. Tim Rix is now in overall charge with John Rix frequently at his desk, taking an interest in the group's various activities and discussing future plans with Tim and others.

Shipping by itself would not have been enough to enable the company to continue and it is successful forays into other activities which has allowed Rix to continue in business as a family concern. Nevertheless, the family have always heeded Bob Rix's advice to be cautious and not to over expand.

Rix Panther in her working environment *[Company archives]*

The Rix Family Tree

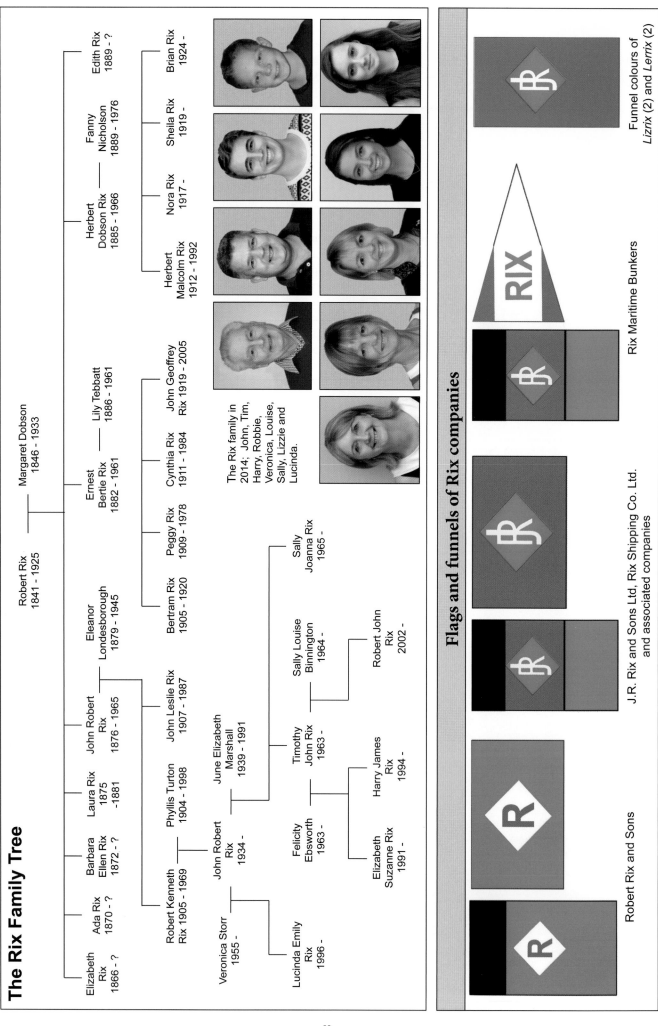

Robert Rix
1841 - 1925 — Margaret Dobson
1846 - 1933

Elizabeth Rix
1866 - ?

Ada Rix
1870 - ?

Barbara Ellen Rix
1872 - ?

Laura Rix
1875 - 1881

John Robert Rix
1876 - 1965 — Eleanor Londesborough
1879 - 1945

Ernest Bertie Rix
1882 - 1961 — Lily Tebbatt
1886 - 1961

Herbert Dobson Rix
1885 - 1966 — Fanny Nicholson
1889 - 1976

Edith Rix
1889 - ?

Phyllis Turton
1904 - 1998 — Robert Kenneth Rix 1905 - 1969

John Leslie Rix
1907 - 1987

Bertram Rix
1905 - 1920

Peggy Rix
1909 - 1978

Cynthia Rix
1911 - 1984

John Geoffrey Rix 1919 - 2005

Herbert Malcolm Rix
1912 - 1992

Nora Rix
1917 -

Sheila Rix
1919 -

Brian Rix
1924 -

John Robert Rix
1934 — June Elizabeth Marshall
1939 - 1991

Veronica Storr
1955 -

Felicity Ebsworth
1963 — Timothy John Rix
1963 -

Sally Louise Binnington
1964 — Sally Joanna Rix
1965 -

Lucinda Emily Rix
1996 -

Elizabeth Suzanne Rix
1991 -

Harry James Rix
1994 -

Robert John Rix
2002 -

The Rix family in 2014; John, Tim, Harry, Robbie, Veronica, Louise, Sally, Lizzie and Lucinda.

Flags and funnels of Rix companies

Robert Rix and Sons

J.R. Rix and Sons Ltd, Rix Shipping Co. Ltd. and associated companies

Rix Maritime Bunkers

Funnel colours of *Lizrix* (2) and *Lerrix* (2)

Seventy five years of Rix motor coasters
Top left: *Robrix* (3), built for the company in 1937. [*World Ship Society Ltd.*]
Top right: *Fylrix*, as completed in 1962: she was later lengthened. [*Company archives*]
Bottom left: *Robrix* (4) acquired in 1985. [*Fotoflite incorporating Skyfotos 373148*]
Bottom right: *Salrix* (2) was bought in 2002 and sold in 2012. [*Fotoflite incorporating Skyfotos 378852*]

Notes on the fleet lists

The first line of each entry gives the ship's name with the notation (1) to (5) to indicate that she is the first to the fifth of that name in the fleet. The dates following are those of entering and leaving the fleet, or when management began and ended. Unless otherwise stated on this line, vessels are steam or motor dry cargo ships with steel hulls.

On the second line is given the ship's official number (O.N.) in the British Register and/or her IMO number; followed by tonnages at acquisition, gross (g) and net (n), plus deadweight (d) if known. The next line gives dimensions: registered length x breadth x draught in feet or, for vessels owned from 1955, the dimensions are length overall x breadth x draught in feet and in metres for vessels owned from 1974 onwards. For any substantial rebuild, new tonnages and dimensions are given on a subsequent line.

For steam and motor ships, the next line describes the engine(s) fitted and names their builder. Steam reciprocating engines may be two-cylinder compound (C. 2-cyl.) or three-cylinder triple-expansion (T. 3-cyl.). For oil engines are given the type where known if different from that of the builder, the number of cylinders, whether two-stroke (2SC) or four-stroke (4SC) cycle, single-acting (SA) or double-acting (DA). Any changes of engine or major modifications are listed, with dates, on the next line. If known from registration documents horsepower figures are given which may be nominal (NHP), indicated (IHP) or brake (BHP), and the ship's speed.

Subsequent lines give the details of the hull builder and then the ship's full career. Where dates of completion are known to the nearest month, they are not quoted if they fall within the same month as the registration date. The port indicated after the title of an owning company is that in which the owners are domiciled. Unless otherwise stated, the ship is registered in the state in which the owning company is based – this increasingly differs from the domicile of the managers. Major non-fatal casualties and all known fates are noted.

The fleet lists are based wherever possible on data in the registration documents of British ships in the National Archives at Kew. Unfortunately, registration documents for ships whose British registry closed after 1955 are not generally available.

Histories are corrected to data published in February 2014.

Robert Rix, Hull
Robert Rix and Sons, Hull

1. R&M 1881-1894 Ketch-rigged wooden auxiliary steamer
O.N. 84641 63g 49n
72.8 x 20.4 x 6.3 feet
C. 2-cyl. by Popely and Harris, Middlesbrough; 18 NHP.
1881: Completed by Robert Rix, Stockton-on-Tees for his own account as R&M.
11.1894: Sold to Welby More, Dunkirk, France.
12.3.1895: Foundered off Beachy Head.
25.3.1895: Register closed.

2. EDITH 1893-1917
O.N. 99488 148g 78n
95.3 x 20.1 x 7.6 feet
1914: 181g 98n
113.0 x 20.1 x 7.6 feet
C. 2-cyl. by Alexander Hall and Company, Aberdeen; 30 NHP.
7.1893: Completed by Alexander Hall and Company, Aberdeen (Yard No. 348).
26.7.1893: Registered in the ownership of Robert Rix and Sons, Hull as EDITH.
1914: Lengthened by about 18 feet.
1.10.1917: Sold to Oakley, Sollas and Co. Ltd., London.
18.12.1917: Sold to the Olwen Steamship Co. Ltd. (Samuel W. Oakley, manager), London.
17.5.1921: Sold to Isaac and Louis Kahn, London.
26.7.1923: Sold to Henry Hillcoat, Norwich.
18.3.1924: Sold to T. Small and Co. (Great Yarmouth) Ltd., Great Yarmouth.
17.12.1931: Sold to the Great Yarmouth Shipping Co. Ltd. (Henry I. Colville, manager), Great Yarmouth.
9.7.1936: Sold to Joseph Barlow (36/64) and John Sinclair (28/64), Dundee, trading as Barlow and Company (Joseph Barlow, manager), Dundee for approximately £750.
6.1951: Demolished at Bo'ness.
20.9.1952: Register closed.

3. WARRENPOINT 1902-1908
O.N. 98271 228g 64n
125.2 x 20.1 x 9.5 feet
C. 2-cyl. by Ross and Duncan, Glasgow; 51 NHP.
24.6.1892: Launched by John Fullerton and Co., Paisley (Yard No. 108).
7.1892: Completed.
5.8.1892: Registered in the ownership of the Carlingford Lough Steamship Co. Ltd. (Joseph Fisher and Sons, manager), Newry as WARRENPOINT.
29.5.1902: Acquired by Robert Rix and Sons, Hull.
28.2.1908: Sank following a collision with the German steamer SCHWALBE (1,178/1898) about 15 miles off the Sunk Light Vessel whilst on a voyage from Boston, Lincolnshire to Dunkirk with a cargo of beans.
10.3.1908: Register closed.

4. PERT 1907-1917
O.N. 99846 171g 61n
105.2 x 20.1 x 8.9 feet
C. 2-cyl. by Ross and Duncan, Glasgow; 28 NHP.
8.1892: Completed by Scott and Son, Bowling (Yard No. 95).
8.9.1892: Registered in the ownership of John Milne and Sons, Montrose as PLOVER.
11.1893: Stranded on Shuna Island, near Oban in Loch Linnhe, and sank.
27.11.1893: Register closed.
1894: Salvaged and repaired.
27.8.1894: Registered in the ownership of Anderson Rodger, Port Glasgow (50/64), James H. Hutchison, Port Glasgow (13/64) and Archibald Sterling (1/64), trading as Sterling and Co., Glasgow.
27.4.1896: Register closed following sale to the Admiralty for use as a dockyard tank vessel and renamed PERT.
22.11.1907: Re-registered in the name of Robert Rix and Sons, Hull.
1.6.1917: Sold to Tom W. Smythe, London.
22.10.1918: Sold to John CRass, Newcastle-upon-Tyne.
9.8.1919: Sold to H.H. Poole and Co. Ltd. (Herbert H. Poole, manager), London.

The company's first steel coaster, *Edith*, aground. *[Company archives]*

The little *Pert* on the Humber. The crane in the background is at Earle's shipyard. *[J. and M. Clarkson collection]*

A fine portrait of the old iron steamer *Owain Tudur* in Rix colours at Bristol. *[J. and M. Clarkson collection]*

5.9.1919: Renamed POOLENA.
22.3.1920: Sold to William Williams and Albert G.M. Cope, Cardiff.
8.9.1920: Sold to the Merches Steamship Co. Ltd. (Ernest J. Williams, manager), Cardiff.
17.11.1921: Struck submerged wreck and sank five miles south east of Minehead whilst on a voyage from Llanelly to Cork with a cargo of coal.
19.12.1921: Register closed.

5. OWAIN TUDUR 1908-1916 Iron
O.N. 86271 238g 89n
125.9 x 20.1 x 10.2 feet
C. 2-cyl by Richard Nevill, Llanelly; 55 NHP.
10.1882: Launched by Samuel Brothers, Llanelly (Yard No. 25).
8.1.1883: Registered in the ownership of the Owain Tudur Steamship Co. Ltd. (Parry Jones and Co., managers), Liverpool as OWAIN TUDUR
18.12.1888: Sold to William Rowland, Runcorn.
26.9.1906: Manager became Alfred Rowland, Liverpool.
27.4.1908: Acquired by Robert Rix and Sons, Hull.
20.5.1908: Transferred to Humber Steam Coasters Ltd. (Robert Rix and Sons, managers), Hull.
15.7.1916: Sold to Harry Parker, Grimsby.
25.6.1919: Transferred to Harry Parker (Grimsby) Ltd., Grimsby.
24.8.1922: Sold to Thomas Grieve junior, Birkenhead.

8.9.1922: Transferred to the Grieve Steamship Co. Ltd. (Thomas Grieve junior, manager), Birkenhead.
18.9.1922: Renamed PEGGY GRIEVE.
13.12.1923: Manager became Duncan MacNicoll, Birkenhead.
26.5.1926: Sold to Bror. Gosta Hulthen, London.
12.9.1929: Sold at Wivenhoe to T.W. Ward Ltd. and broken up by them at Grays, Essex.
28.9.1929: Register closed.

6. SPURNPOINT 1908-1919
O.N. 128110 235g 88n
125.3 x 21.1 x 8.8 feet
C. 2-cyl. by Alexander Hall and Co. Ltd., Aberdeen; 56 NHP.
1952: 2SCSA 6-cyl. oil engine made in 1942 by British Polar Engines Ltd., Glasgow.
29.8.1908: Launched by Alexander Hall and Co. Ltd., Aberdeen (Yard No.445) for Robert Rix and Sons, Hull as SPURNPOINT.
9.1908: Completed.
8.1919: Sold to the Elvedon Shipping Co. Ltd. (Ernest G. Griffin, manager), Cardiff.
1920: Sold to Scorrier Steam Coasters Ltd. (John H. Woods, manager), Cardiff.
9.1927: Sold to William J. Ireland, Liverpool and renamed QUICKTHORN.
4.1931: Sold to Buchan and Hogg, Grangemouth and renamed DUNAVON.
1941: Transferred to the Dunavon Steamship Company (Buchan and Hogg Ltd., managers), Grangemouth.
12.1945: Sold to William R. Metcalfe, Falmouth.

1952: Sold to John Wilson, London and re-engined.
1952: Transferred to Lockett, Wilson Ltd., London.
1954: Sold to the Arlesford Trading Co. Ltd., London.
9.7.1955: Arrived at Llanelli for demolition by Rees Shipbreaking Co.

7. SAXON QUEEN 1912-1916
O.N. 118127 276g 95n
130.0 x 22.2 x 9.8 feet
C. 2-cyl. by Richardsons Westgarth and Co. Ltd., Middlesbrough; 70 NHP, 10 knots.
8.1904: Completed by Langeveld & van Vliet, Hardinxveld, Netherlands (Yard No. 27).
12.9.1904: Registered in the ownership of the Gale Shipping Co. Ltd. (Joseph Gale, manager), Liverpool as HURRICANE.
23.3.1909: Sold to Shipping Investments Ltd. (Charles H. Pile manager), London.
27.1.1911: Sold to the London and Channel Islands Steamship Co. Ltd. (Cheeswright and Ford, managers), London.
28.1.1911: Renamed SAXON QUEEN.
25.7.1912: Acquired by the Saxon Queen Steamship Co. Ltd. (Robert Rix and Sons, managers), Hull.
10.2.1915: Transferred to Humber Steam Coasters Ltd. (Robert Rix and Sons, managers), Hull.
19.10.1916: Wrecked in Ukanski Bay during Admiralty requisition whilst on a voyage from Hull to Archangel with a cargo of Government stores and general cargo.
20.8.1917: Register closed.

Spurnpoint at Bristol. *[J. and M. Clarkson collection]*

Saxon Queen, built in the Netherlands as *Hurricane* and seen as this at Preston around 1908. *[J. and M. Clarkson collection]*

8. TAFFY 1913-1914

O.N. 102368 173g 90n
100.5 x 21.1 x 9.3 feet
C. 2-cyl. by David J. Dunlop and Co., Port Glasgow; 37 NHP, 8 knots.
19.6.1894: Launched by David J. Dunlop and Co., Port Glasgow (Yard No. 224).
10.7.1894: Registered in the ownership of John Brundrit, Runcorn as TAFFY.
14.4.1895: Transferred to the Taffy Steamship Co. Ltd. (Brundrit and Co., managers), Runcorn.
7.4.1898: Manager became George W. Hayes, Liverpool.
21.12.1898: Sold to Charles Page and Edward C. Turner, Blakeney, Norfolk.
5.8.1913: Acquired by Robert Rix and Sons, Hull.
1.12.1914: Sold to the Blackrock and Passage Railway, Cork.
17.11.1916: Foundered about eight miles south of St. Govan's Head, Pembrokeshire whilst on a voyage from Cardiff to Cork with a cargo of coal.
22.11.1916: Register closed.

9. ARDNAGRENA 1914-1919

O.N. 124673 223g 88n
125.0 x 22.1 x 8.1 feet
C.2-cyl. by Renfrew Brothers and Co., Irvine; 42 NHP.
12.8.1908: Launched by George Brown and Co., Greenock (Yard No. 50) for James Waterson, Ardnagrena, County Antrim, as ARDNAGRENA.
9.1908: Completed.
2.1914: Acquired by Humber Steam

Coasters Ltd. (Robert Rix and Sons, managers), Hull.
4.1919: Sold to H.H. Poole and Co. (Shipping) Ltd., London.
6.1920: Sold to the Isle of Man Steam Packet Co. Ltd., Douglas, Isle of Man and renamed CUSHAG.
2.1943: Sold to Williamstown Shipping Co. Ltd. (Comben Longstaff and Co. Ltd., managers), London.
10.1943: Sold to Roderick Cunningham, Scalpay.
5.1947: Sold to John R. Bremner and Co., Stromness, Orkney.
9.1953: Sold to Barlow and Co. (Dundee)

Ltd. (Joseph Barlow, manager), Dundee.
28.5.1957: Arrived at Granton for breaking up by Malcolm Brechin.

10. MAGRIX (1) 1916-1937

O.N. 139306 314g 124n
135.3 x 23.1 x 9.5 feet
T.3-cyl. by Hall, Russell and Co. Ltd., Aberdeen in November 1900; 57 NHP.
14.9.1916: Launched by Cochrane and Sons Ltd., Selby (Yard No. 723).
12.1916: Completed for Robert Rix and Sons, Hull as MAGRIX.
5.1937: Sold to Alexander M. Massie, Aberdeen and renamed DEEDON.

Cushag, the former *Ardnagrena*. *[World Ship Society Ltd.]*

1942: Managers became Rose Line Ltd., Sunderland.
7.1946: Transferred to the Deeside Shipping Co. Ltd. (Thomas Rose and Co., managers), Sunderland.
8.1955: Sold to Bremner and Co. (John R. Bremner, manager), Stromness.
12.1955: Renamed ORKNEY DAWN.
25.1.1957: Arrived at Passage West, County Cork for demolition by Haulbowline Industries Ltd.

11. ROBRIX (1) 1916-1929
O.N. 139307 314g 124n
135.3 x 23.1 x 9.5 feet
T.3-cyl. made in 1900 and rebuilt by Drypool Engineering Co. (Hull) Ltd., Hull; 50 NHP, 7 knots.
14.9.1916: Launched by Cochrane and Sons Ltd., Selby (Yard No. 724).
21.12.1916: Registered in the ownership of Humber Steam Coasters Ltd. (Robert Rix and Sons, managers), Hull as ROBRIX.
1.1917: Completed.
14.4.1929: Sank after colliding with the steamer ANDELLE (1,832/1922) in fog off Haisboro', approximately two miles south south east of Newarp Light Vessel, in position 52.45.30 north, 01.54.30 east. She was on a voyage from Hull to Teignmouth with a cargo of oil cake and meal. One member of her crew was lost.
30.5.1929: Register closed.

12. JARRIX (1) 1917-1939
O.N. 139308 429g 203n
150.2 x 24.6 x 11.0 feet
T. 3-cyl. by Shields Engineering and Dry Dock Co. Ltd., North Shields; 69 NHP, 430 IHP, 9 knots.
28.10.1916: Launched by Cochrane and Sons Ltd., Selby (Yard No.726).
30.12.1916: Registered in the ownership of Humber Steam Coasters Ltd. (Robert Rix and Sons Ltd., managers), Hull as JARRIX.
2.1917: Completed.
26.5.1939: Sold to the Ribble Shipping Co. Ltd. (William J. Ireland, manager), Liverpool.
2.8.1939: Renamed GORSETHORN.
7.12.1940: Disabled and abandoned 14 miles off the Bar Light Vessel, Liverpool Bay whilst on a voyage from Preston to Cork with a cargo of coal.
9.12.1940: Foundered whilst under tow about one mile west by north of the Bar Light Vessel.
4.2.1942: Register closed.

13. EBBRIX (1) 1917-1939
O.N. 139311 429g 203n
150.2 x 24.6 x 11.0 feet
T.3-cyl. by Shields Engineering and Dry Dock Co. Ltd., North Shields. 69 NHP, 8 knots.
11.11.1916: Launched by Cochrane and Sons, Selby (Yard No.727).
23.1.1917: Registered in the ownership of Robert Rix and Sons, Hull as EBBRIX.

Magrix (1) was built in 1916 with a 16-year old steam engine. *[Company archives]*

Robrix (1) was also fitted with second-hand engines. *[J. and M. Clarkson collection]*

Jarrix (1). *[J. and M. Clarkson collection]*

Ebbrix. [Roy Fenton collection]

3.1917: Completed.
30.6.1939: Sold to the Ribble Shipping
Co. Ltd. (William J. Ireland, manager),
Liverpool.
31.8.1939: Renamed BANNTHORN.
6.11.1942: Sold to the Springfal Shipping
Co. Ltd., London.
5.12.1946: Renamed SPRINGOUSE.
28.1.1947: Sold to the Ribble Shipping
Co. Ltd. (William J. Ireland, manager),
Liverpool.
18.3.1947: Renamed BANNTHORN.
17.9.1947: Sold to Thomas Stone (Shipping)
Ltd., Swansea.
5.8.1949: Renamed BROOKSTONE.
11.2.1950: Sold to S. William Coe and Co.
Ltd., Liverpool.
10.6.1950: Renamed BANNTHORN.
9.11.1950: Transferred to the Thorn
Line Ltd. (S. William Coe and Co. Ltd.,
managers), Liverpool.
8.10.1954: Arrived at Troon to be broken up
by the West of Scotland Shipbreaking Co.
Ltd.
9.2.1955: Register closed.

14. HADRIX 1919-1920
O.N. 139333 570g 252n
164.8 x 27.0 x 11.1 feet
T.3-cyl. by John Lewis and Sons Ltd.,
Aberdeen; 105 NHP.
1919: Completed by John Lewis and Sons
Ltd., Aberdeen (Yard No. 54) for Robert Rix
and Sons, Hull as HADRIX.
1920: Sold to Onesimus Dorey and Sons,
St. Peter Port, Guernsey and renamed
LAKEWOOD.
1923: Transferred to the Sea Transportation
Co. Ltd. (Onesimus Dorey and Sons,
managers), St. Peter Port, Guernsey.
1930: Transferred to Onesimus Dorey and

Lakewood, formerly *Hadrix,* at Falmouth in Dorey colours on 18th July 1932. [J. and
M. Clarkson collection]

Sons, later Onesimus Dorey and Sons Ltd.,
St. Peter Port, Guernsey.
25.5.1956: Sailed from the Tyne after boiler
repairs but suffered a further breakdown at
Immingham and it was decided to sell her
for demolition.
1956: Sold to British Iron and Steel
Corporation (BISCO) and allocated to
Clayton and Davie Ltd.
7.6.1956 Arrived at Dunston for demolition
in tow of GUARDSMAN (329/1946).

15. NORRIX (1) 1920-1921
O.N. 144043 576g 283n
165.0 x 27.0 x 11.0 feet
T.3-cyl. by Earle's Shipbuilding and

Engineering Co. Ltd., Hull in 1904, rebuilt by
Drypool Engineering Co. Ltd., Hull in 1920.
12.1919: Launched by Cochrane and Sons
Ltd., Selby (Yard No. 690).
26.1.1920: Completed.
9.4.1920: Registered in the ownership of
Robert Rix and Sons, Hull as NORRIX.
26.3.1921: Capsized and sank after striking
the Mole at Zeebrugge during a voyage from
Par to Antwerp with a cargo of china clay.
12.10.1921: Register closed

16. MAYRIX 1920-1934
O.N. 144055 794g 375n
185.1 x 31.0 x 11.7 feet
T.3-cyl. by Earle's Shipbuilding and

The short-lived *Norrix* (1) of 1920. *[Company archives]*

Engineering Co., Ltd., Hull; 111 NHP,
9.5 knots.
20.5.1920: Launched by Cochrane and
Sons Ltd., Selby (Yard No. 697).
9.9.1920: Registered in the ownership
of Humber Steam Coasters Ltd.
(Robert Rix and Sons, managers), Hull
as MAYRIX.
15.1.1934: Sold to H. Harrison
(Shipping) Ltd., London.
24.1.1934: Renamed KEMPTON.
4.1.1937: Sold to the Polgarth
Steamship Co. Ltd. (Pollexfen and Co.
Ltd., managers), Liverpool.
22.1.1937: Renamed POLGARTH.
1.3.1942: Mined and sunk two miles
south south west of Aldeburgh Light
Float in position 52.09 north, 01.42.33
east whilst on a voyage from Blyth
to Southampton with a cargo of 856
tons of coal. The crew of sixteen was
saved.
9.4.1942: Register closed.

17. KENRIX (1) 1921-1945
O.N. 144079 692g 317n
175.0 x 29.1 x 11.3 feet
T. 3-cyl. by John Lewis and Sons Ltd.,
Aberdeen; 96 NHP, 9 knots.
27.11.1920: Launched by Cochrane
and Sons Ltd., Selby (Yard No. 701).
5.1921: Completed.
20.7.1921: Registered in the ownership
of Robert Rix and Sons, Hull as
KENRIX.
23.11.1945: Sold to the Polpen
Shipping Co. Ltd. (Hannan, Samuel
and Co. Ltd., managers), Fowey.

Two views of *Mayrix*. In that above she still carries steadying sails. *[World Ship Society Ltd., Company archives]*

Ernrix of 1921 at Poole. *[Roy Griffin/World Ship Society Ltd.]*

4.2.1946: Renamed POLKERRIS.
1946: Managers became Samuel Hough and Co. (Shipping) Ltd., Falmouth.
31.12.1953: Arrived at Dunston-on-Tyne for breaking up by C.W. Dorkin and Co. Ltd.
14.6.1954: Register closed

18. ERNRIX 1921-1939
O.N. 144090 692g 317n
175.0 x 29.1 x 11.3 feet
T. 3-cyl. by John Lewis and Sons Ltd., Aberdeen; 96 NHP, 600 IHP, 9 knots.
27.11.1920: Launched by Cochrane and Sons Ltd., Selby (Yard No. 702).
30.9.1921: Registered in the ownership of Humber Steam Coasters Ltd. (Robert Rix and Sons, managers), Hull as ERNRIX.
23.6.1939: Sprang a leak and foundered one and a half miles west north west of Saltscar Buoy, Tees Bar in position 54.39.10 north, 01.03.48 west whilst on a voyage from Hull to Thornaby-on-Tees with a cargo of wheat. The crew of ten was rescued.
18.8.1939: Register closed.

19. NORRIX (2) 1922-1930
O.N. 136201 272g 101n
119.4 x 23.4 x 8.3 feet
C. 2-cyl. by J.P. Rennoldson and Sons Ltd., South Shields.
26.5.1914: Launched by J.P. Rennoldson and Sons Ltd., South Shields (Yard No. 290).
21.7.1914: Registered in the ownership of D. Hurtley and Sons Ltd., Hull as ABUS.
9.7.1918: Sold to James Kell, Sunderland.
12.4.1922: Sold to John B. Forster, Sunderland

Middle and bottom: *Kenrix* (1) of 1921. *[World Ship Society Ltd., Roy Fenton collection]*

6.11.1922: Acquired by Robert Rix and Sons, Hull.
27.11.1922: Renamed NORRIX.
30.10.1930: Sold to the Wilson Steamship Co. Ltd. (T.W. Dixon, manager), Whitehaven.
5.12.1930: Renamed CUMBRIA
2.4.1954: Sold to William Bennett, Killylegh, County Down (John B. Moffat and Co., Workington, managers).
1.7.1955: Arrived at Troon to be broken up by the West of Scotland Shipbreaking Co. Ltd.
5.10.1955: Register closed.

20. MALRIX 1923-1940
O.N. 147086 703g 354n
175.1 x 29.0 x 11.4 feet
T. 3-cyl. by C.D. Holmes and Co. Ltd., Hull; 96 NHP, 9 knots.
19.4.1923: Launched by Cochrane and Sons Ltd., Selby (Yard No. 788).
20.6.1923: Registered in the ownership of Rix Steamships Ltd. (Robert Rix and Sons, managers), Hull as MALRIX.
17.12.1940: Mined and sunk off Southend one and three quarter miles south by west of the Nore Light Vessel whilst on a voyage from Hull to London with 781 tons of coal. Eight of her crew of twelve were lost.
22.1.1941: Register closed.
9-10.1942: Wreck removed.

21. LESRIX (1) 1924-1941
O.N. 147126 703g 354n 900d
175.1 x 29.0 x 11.4 feet
T. 3-cyl. by C.D. Holmes and Co. Ltd., Hull; 96 NHP, 9 knots.
16.5.1923: Launched by Cochrane and Sons Ltd., Selby (Yard No. 789).
11.1.1924: Registered in the ownership of Rix Steamships Ltd. (Robert Rix and Sons, managers), Hull as LESRIX.
8.9.1941: Sold to the Williamstown Shipping Co. Ltd. (Comben Longstaff and Co. Ltd., managers), London.
26.1.1942: Stranded at Hackney Head, two miles north of the River Ythan, near Cruden, Aberdeenshire whilst on a voyage from Sunderland to Belfast and Cardiff with a cargo of machinery. Four of the crew of fourteen were rescued using Breeches Buoy.
7.5.1942: Register closed.

22. PEGRIX (1) 1928-1936
O.N. 144851 270g 99n
117.1 x 22.2 x 9.1 feet
C. 2-cyl. by Shields Engineering and Drydock Co. Ltd., North Shields; 57 NHP.
11.1921: Completed by R.B. Harrison and Sons Ltd., Newcastle-upon-Tyne (Yard No. 2) for the Wear Steam Shipping Co. (1917) Ltd. (Thomas Rose, manager), Sunderland as MOORSIDE.

Wilson's *Cumbria,* formerly the second *Norrix.* *[B. and A. Feilden/J. and M. Clarkson collection]*

Malrix at Poole, 7th August 1939. *[Roy Griffin/J. and M. Clarkson collection]*

Lesrix (1) passing under the Clifton Suspension Bridge on the River Avon. *[York Series/J. and M. Clarkson collection]*

1928: Acquired by Robert Rix and Sons, Hull and renamed PEGRIX.
1936: Sold to the Ramsey Steamship Co. Ltd. (J. Ramsey, manager), Ramsey, Isle of Man and renamed BEN ELLAN.
6.7.1961: Sold to Hammond Lane Foundry, Dublin for demolition.
8.7.1961: Work commenced.

23. ROBRIX (2)/NORBRITT 1930-1940
O.N. 140523 287g 104n
120.1 x 23.6 x 10.3 feet
C. 2-cyl. by Shields Engineering Co. Ltd., North Shields; 64 NHP, 9 knots.
7.1917: Completed by the Ardrossan Drydock and Shipbuilding Co. Ltd., Ardrossan (Yard No. 273).
9.7.1917: Registered in the ownership of Joseph Monks and Co. Ltd., Warrington as LILLENA.
29.4.1919: Sold to R.S. Dalgleish Ltd., Newcastle-upon-Tyne, who intended to rename her SPEEDWELL but this was never carried out.
15.7.1919: Sold to Thomas E. Brooke, trading as T.G. Beatley and Son, London.
15.9.1919: Renamed MADAME LUNDI.
9.9.1921: Renamed WHITGIFT.
22.11.1921: Sold to the Channel Steamship Co. Ltd. (John B. Bennett, manager), London.
17.10.1930: Acquired by Robert Rix and Sons, Hull.
20.11.1930: Renamed ROBRIX.
9.3.1936: Transferred to Brittain Coasters Ltd. (Arthur T. Jackson, manager), Brighton.
18.4.1936: Renamed NORBRITT.
21.5.1940: Sold to Challis, Stern and Co. Ltd. (Arthur A. Jackson, manager), London.
30.7.1946: Renamed WARREN COURT.
9.5.1952: Transferred to the Warren Shipping Co. Ltd. (Ernest E. Scott, manager), London.
1953: Sold to the British Iron and Steel Corporation (BISCO).
13.4.1953: Delivered to C.W. Dorkin and Co. Ltd., Gateshead.
6.1953: Demolition commenced.
18.10.1953: Register closed.

24. NORRIX (3) 1936-1945
O.N. 162495 IMO 5102932
264g 130n
117.0 x 23.2 x 9.0 feet
4SCSA 4-cyl. oil engine by Motorenfabrik 'Deutz' A.G., Köln, Germany.
6.1948: 4SCSA 5-cyl. oil engine by R.A. Lister (Marine Sales) Ltd., Dursley.
1965: 4SCSA 6- cyl. oil engine by the Caterpillar Tractor Co., Peoria, Illinois, USA.

Pegrix (1) sailing from Aberystwyth. *[Company archives]*

Middle and bottom: two views of *Norbritt*, the lower dated 29th August 1936. *[York Series/J. and M. Clarkson collection, Roy Fenton collection]*

10.1930: Completed by N.V. Scheepswerf 'Gideon', J. Koster Hzn., Groningen, Netherlands (Yard No. 128) for Thomas J. Metcalf, London as ELLEN M.

1936: Acquired by Robert Rix and Sons, Hull and renamed NORRIX.

1945: Sold to Martin's Coastal Steamships Ltd. (Charles E.C. Martin, manager), London.

1946: Renamed DARTMEET.

1947: Sold to the Plym Shipping Co. Ltd., Plymouth and renamed PLYMPTON.

1948: Sold to the Mountwood Shipping Co. Ltd., Liverpool, re-engined, and renamed TORWOOD.

1959: Sold to William G. Dennison, Kirkwall and renamed ELWICK BAY.

1960: Transferred to the Elwick Bay Shipping Co. Ltd., Kirkwall.

1965: Re-engined.

3.1978: Arrived at Aberdeen and laid up at Regent Quay where she remained without moving until 1981. Whilst laid up she was sold several times, and for a time both the vessel and owning company belonged to G. Dupenois Shipping Ltd. Her final recorded owner was Batty (Towage and Salvage) Ltd.

1981: Sold by Aberdeen Harbour Board to meet harbour dues to David Stewart (Metals) Ltd., Aberdeen for demolition.

5.1981: Broken up on the pontoon dock in the Albert Basin, Aberdeen.

25. ROBRIX (3) 1937-1963

O.N. 165661 292g 124n
125.2 x 24.0 8.5 feet
4SCSA 6-cyl. oil engine by Humboldt-Deutzmotoren A.G., Köln-Deutz, Germany.

5.1937: Completed by N.V. Scheepswerf 'Gideon', J. Koster Hzn., Groningen, Netherlands (Yard No.154) for Robert Rix and Sons, Hull as ROBRIX.

3.12.1940: Struck a mine two miles from Spurn Point Lighthouse after leaving Immingham for London with a cargo of coal. Reached Grimsby in a sinking condition. Subsequently repaired and returned to service.

6.1963: Sold to William J. Sutton, Croydon, Surrey for £13,000 and renamed PURSUIT.

1967: Sold to Equity (Home Counties) Ltd., London.

1968: Sold to Elea Shipping Co. Ltd., Nicosia, Cyprus and renamed NETTUNO.

17.5.1968: Arrested at Hull, and later sold by the Admiralty Marshall to Hughes Bolckow Ltd.

23.3.1969: Arrived at Blyth for demolition, but resold to Offshore Oil Rig Services Ltd., St. Helier, Jersey and renamed YOUNG ANN.

1972: Sold to G. King and Sons Ltd., Great Yarmouth for demolition but resold.

4.1974: Arrived at Victoria Dock Slipway, Hull for breaking up by Albert Draper and Son Ltd., Hull.

The former *Norrix* (3) in later life as *Torwood* at Liverpool (top), and as *Elwick Bay* on the Ouse near Goole (middle) with modified masts, a new wheelhouse and a crane on deck. *[J. and M.Clarkson collection, Roy Cressey]*

Robrix (3) off Dover. *[FotoFlite incorporating Skyfotos/Company archives]*

26. PEGRIX (2) 1938-1941

O.N. 165705 296g 120n
125.2 x 23.9 x 8.6 feet
4SCSA 6-cyl. oil engine by Humbolt-Deutzmotoren A.G., Köln, Germany; 300 BHP, 9 knots.

5.1938: Completed by N.V. Scheepswerf 'Gideon', J. Koster Hzn., Groningen, Netherlands (Yard No 164).

2.5.1938: Registered in the ownership of Humber Steam Coasters Ltd. (Robert Rix and Sons, Hull, managers), Hull as PEGRIX.

21.8.1941: Collided with the steamer NORMANDY COAST (1,428/1916) north east of Cromer and sank in position 53.03.30 north, 01.38 east. She was on a voyage from Rochester to Lossiemouth with a cargo of cement in bags.

2.9.1941: Register closed.

Pegrix (2) lasted for only three years so there are few illustrations of her. This is probably a builder's photograph. *[Company archives]*

27. MAGRIX (2) 1938-1947

O.N. 165742 IMO 5026798 454g 222n
165.3 x 25.8 x 8.8 feet
4SCSA 8-cyl. oil engine by Humboldt-Deutzmotoren A.G., Köln-Deutz, Germany; 94 NHP.

3.1949: 4SCSA 8-cyl. oil engine built 1937 by Humboldt-Deutzmotoren A.G., Köln-Deutz; 49 NHP.

8.1938: Completed by N.V. Scheepswerf 'Gideon', J. Koster Hzn., Groningen, Netherlands (Yard No. 165) for Robert Rix and Sons, Hull as MAGRIX.

1947: Transferred to J.R. Rix and Sons, Hull.

1949: Re-engined.

1957: Transferred to J.R. Rix and Sons Ltd., Hull.

1960: Sold to F.A. Ashmead and Son Ltd., Bristol and renamed ASHLEIGH.

1964: Sold to Alex A. Zissis and others (John Prassinos, managers), Piraeus, Greece and renamed LEONIDAS.

Pre-war (above) and post-war (below) views of *Magrix* (2), the upper probably taken whilst on trials. *[Roy Fenton collection; World Ship Society Ltd.]*

1971: Sold to Paraskeva Brothers, Volos, Greece and renamed LAMBRINI.
1978: Managers became Vita Management S.A., Piraeus.
1979: Managers became A. and N. Papageorgiou, Volos.
1980: Managers became Nikolaos Adamakis, Piraeus.
1981: Sold for demolition to Kinopraxis K. Spiliopoulos, her main engine having been removed during 12.1980.
3.1981: Demolition began at Perama.

28. BRIXHAM/EBBRIX (2) 1939-1960
O.N. 166577 258g 157n
136.5 x 23.6 x 8.4 feet
4SCSA 4-cyl. oil engine by Motorenwerke Mannheim A.G., Mannheim, Germany; 49 NHP.
1951: 2SCSA 5-cyl. oil engine by Crossley Brothers Ltd., Manchester; 50 NHP.
1965: 2SCSA 8-cyl. oil engine by Bergius-Kelvin Co. Ltd., Glasgow; 320 BHP, 9.5 knots.
9.1938: Completed by A. Vuijk and Zonen, Capelle a/d Ysel, Netherlands (Yard No. 647) for H. Harrison (Shipping) Ltd.,

London as BRIXHAM.
1939: Acquired by Robert Rix and Sons, Hull.
1940: Renamed EBBRIX.
1951: Re-engined.
1960: Sold to Hazely Ltd., St. Peter Port, Guernsey and renamed ORSELINA.
1965: Re-engined.
1966: Managers became Continental Cargoes Ltd., Rochford.
1969: Sold to Burry Sand Co. Ltd., Llanelli and converted to a sand carrier.
1972: Sold to Isaac Jones, Llanelli for demolition.
11.1972: Breaking up began at Llanelli.

Middle and bottom: *Ebbrix* (2), the lower photograph taken 13th August 1949. *[Company archives; World Ship Society Ltd.]*

29. NORRIX (4) 1946-1963

O.N. 166693 I.M.O. 5405396 325g 146n
137.0 x 24.6 x 8.8 feet
2SCSA 6-cyl. oil engine by Crossley Brothers
Ltd., Manchester; 330 BHP, 9 knots.
7.5.1943: Launched by Richards Ironworks
Ltd., Lowestoft (Yard No. 310) for the
Ministry of War Transport, London (Robert
Rix and Sons, Hull, managers) as EMPIRE
SPORTSMAN.
9.1943: Completed.
1946: Acquired by Robert Rix and Sons,
Hull and renamed NORRIX.
10.1961: Engine refitted.
1963: Sold to N.T. Giannoutsos, Piraeus,
Greece for £14,000 and renamed IONION.
1966: Sold to P. Vrachopoulos and M.
Pataka (A. Rigopoulos, manager), Piraeus.
1977: Sold to Demetrios Patakas, Piraeus.
1982: Sold to Georgios Odysseas
Charalabous, Mytilene, Greece.
1985: Transferred to Georgios Odysseas and
Maria Pataka Charalabous, Mytilene.
5.1985: Broken up at Perama.

> **J.R. Rix and Sons, Hull**
> **Rix Shipping Co. Ltd., Hull**
> **J.R. Rix and Sons Ltd., Hull**

MAGRIX (2) 1947-1960
See 27 above

30. KENRIX (2) 1950-1958

O.N. 165074 511g 245n
158.6 x 25.6 x 9.8 feet
4SCSA 6-cyl. oil engine by Motorenfabriken
'Deutz' A.G., Köln-Deutz, Germany; 70 NHP.
1950: 4SCSA 8-cyl. oil engine made in 1938
by Humboldt-Deutz Motoren A.G., Colgart,
Germany; 71 NHP.
1953: 2SCSA 6-cyl. oil engine by Crossley
Brothers Ltd., Manchester; 60 NHP.
1931: Completed by N.V. Scheepsbouwwerf
Gebroeder Pot, Bolnes, Netherlands (Yard
No. 845) for N.V. Motorship 'Maraboe'
(H. Voskamp, managers), Rotterdam,

Two views of *Norrix* (4). *[W.H. Brown/J. and M.Clarkson collection; Company archives]*

Netherlands as MARABOE.
1933: Managers became Gebroeder
Voskamp Technisch Bureau, Rotterdam.
1936: Sold to William A. Wilson,
Southampton and renamed NGARUA.
1937: Sold to James Fisher and Sons Ltd.,
Barrow-in-Furness and renamed LOCH
FISHER.
1946: Sold to T. Bagley and Co. Ltd.,
Middlesbrough and renamed ROXTON.
1950: Acquired by Rix Shipping Co. Ltd.
(J.R. Rix and Sons, managers), Hull and
renamed KENRIX.
1957: Managers J.R. Rix and Sons Ltd., Hull.
1958: Sold to C.D. and C. Ventouris and N.
Diakos (Cleovoulos Ventouris, manager),
Piraeus, Greece and renamed KIMOLOS.
1961: Sold to Constantinos Georgis
Ventouris, Piraeus.
8.11.1963: Sank off Odensholm Island in the
Baltic while on a voyage from Sunderland to
Leningrad in ballast. Her crew was rescued
by the Russian salvage vessel HERMES and
landed at Tallinn.

31. JARRIX (2) 1950-1955

O.N. 183432 IMO 5371193 551g 326n
170.5 x 28.5 x 9.7 feet
2SCSA 8-cyl. Deutz-type oil engine by

Nydquist & Holm A/B, Trollhattan, Sweden;
91 NHP.
3.1956: 4SCSA 6-cyl. oil engine by
Motorenfabriek 'Deutz' A.G., Köln-Deutz,
West Germany; 800 BHP, 12.5 knots.
24.10.1946: Launched by Kalmar Varv,
Kalmar, Sweden (Yard No. 356).
4.1947: Completed for Rederiaktieb
Ruth (Leopold Glucksman, manager),
Gothenburg, Sweden as ARNE.
18.3.1950: Registered in the ownership of J.R.
Rix and Sons, Hull as JARRIX.
20.4.1955: Sold to William Robertson
Shipowners Ltd. (William Robertson,
Glasgow, managers), Glasgow and later
renamed TURQUOISE.
1958: Transferred to Gem Line Ltd. (William
Robertson Ltd., managers), Glasgow.
1966: Sold to Helena Theodora Vavatsioula
and others, Thessaloniki, Greece and
renamed HELLENIKOS VORRAS.
1972: Managers became G.M. Moundreas
and Brothers, Piraeus, Greece.
1979: Sold to Georgios Hatzielenis, Piraeus
and renamed GEORGIOS.
1982: Sold to Green Parrot S.A., Panama
and renamed PAOLA X.
7.2001: Deleted from 'Lloyd's Register' as
continued existence in doubt.

Two second-hand ships were purchased in 1950, the British coaster *Roxton* and the Swedish *Arne*.

The *Roxton* was renamed *Kenrix* (2) (top) and was part of the fleet for eight years until her sale to Greece.

The *Arne* became the *Jarrix* (2) (above) and remained in the fleet for only five years before her sale to other British owners. Later she passed through the hands of various Greek owners, holding the name *Georgios* from 1979 to 1982 (right). *[Company archives]*

32. LESRIX (2) 1954-1960
O.N. 185172 590g 361n 730d
177.2 x 28.8 x 10.3 feet
4SCSA 6-cyl. oil engine by Société
d'Elecricité and de Mecanique (Thomson-
Houston et Carels) S.A., Ghent, Belgium;
43 NHP.
10.1938: Completed by Beliard Crighton et
Compagnie (Belgium) S.A., Ostend, Belgium
(Yard No. 74) for Armement Alexander,
Antwerp, Belgium as FRANCINE.
1940: Captured by German forces while
lying at Cockerill's Hoboken shipyard.
21.8.1944: Scuttled at Bayonne to avoid
capture by Allied forces.
1946: Salvaged, repaired and returned to
Armement Alexander, Antwerp.
1954: Acquired by J.R. Rix and Sons, Hull
and renamed LESRIX.
1957: Transferred to J.R. Rix and Sons Ltd.,
Hull.
29.10.1960: Sailed from Goole for Hayle
with a cargo of coal and disappeared. She is
believed to have sunk off the Isle of Wight
around 31.10.1960.

33. BOBRIX (1) 1957-1970
O.N. 186735 IMO 5047003 540g 276n 780d
179.8 x 28.8 x 12.0 feet
1968: 647g 347n 950d
202.3 x 28.8 x 12.0 feet
2SCSA 6-cyl. oil engine by Crossley Brothers
Ltd., Manchester; 510 BHP, 10.5 knots.
24.11.1956: Launched by N.V. Scheepswerf
'Gideon', J. Koster Hzn., Groningen,
Netherlands (Yard No. 237) for J.R. Rix and
Sons, Hull, as BOBRIX.
2.1957: Completed.
1957: Transferred to J.R. Rix and Sons Ltd.,
Hull.
1968: Lengthened.
1970: Transferred to Highseas Ltd. (J.R. Rix
and Sons Ltd., managers), Hull.

Top: The Belgian-built *Lesrix* (2). *[FotoFlite incorporating Skyfotos/Company archives]*
Middle: *Bobrix* (1) as built. *[FotoFlite incorporating Skyfotos/Company archives]*
Bottom: *Bobrix* (1) after lengthening and without derricks. *[World Ship Society Ltd.]*

14.12.1981: Sank off the Channel Islands in position 49.27.30 north, 03.27.30 west after taking on water when her hatch covers became dislodged during a force 10 gale during a voyage from Bordeaux to Teignmouth with a cargo of maize. A helicopter from RAF Culdrose had lifted off her crew of six the previous evening.

34. JONRIX (1) 1957-1973
O.N. 186752 584g 276n 780d
179.8 x 28.8 x 12.0 feet
1968: 647g 347n 950d
202.3 x 28.8 x 12.0 feet
2SCSA 6-cyl. oil engine by Crossley Brothers Ltd., Manchester; 510 BHP, 10.5 knots
6.4.1957: Launched by N.V. Scheepswerf 'Gideon', J. Koster Hzn., Groningen, Netherlands, (Yard No. 238) for Rix Shipping Co. Ltd. (J.R. Rix and Sons Ltd., managers), Hull as JONRIX.
6.1957: Completed.
1968: Lengthened.
20.4.1973: Sank near the Outer Ruytingen Buoy, ten miles off Dunkirk, in position 51.14 north, 02.07 east whilst on a voyage from Plymouth to Antwerp after her cargo of china clay shifted in severe weather. The eight crew, plus two children and their mother, were picked up by the German motor vessel NAUTICA (498/1963). An injured crew member was flown to Ramsgate.

35. KENRIX (3) 1960-1984
O.N. 301624 IMO 5185257
592g 357n 800d
188.7 x 28.3 x 11.7 feet
1967: 635g 413n 925d
203.1 x 28.3 x 11.7 feet
2SCSA 5-cyl. oil engine made in 1952 by Crossley Brothers Ltd., Manchester; 560 BHP, 10.5 knots.
1967: 2SCSA 8-cyl. oil engine by Drypool Engineering and Dry Dock Co. Ltd., Hull; 660 BHP.
12.9.1959: Launched by v/h A. Apol C.V. Scheepswerf 'Appingedam', Appingedam, Netherlands (Yard No. 185) for J.R. Rix and Sons Ltd., Hull as KENRIX.
2.1960: Completed.
1965: Transferred to the Whitehaven Shipping Co. Ltd. (J.R. Rix and Sons Ltd., managers), Hull.
1967: Lengthened and re-engined.
1984: Sold to Wm. Dennison (Shapinsay) Ltd., Kirkwall and renamed DEER SOUND.
1987: Transferred to Dennison Shipping Ltd., Kirkwall.
1988: Sold to Angel Sea Marine Co. Ltd., Valletta, Malta and renamed MADI.
1989: Sold to Hesperia Shipping Co. S.A., Panama and registered in Honduras.
1990: Sold to Fatme Mostafa El Jundi, Piraeus, Greece and renamed ASRA, retaining Honduras registry.

Jonrix (1) sailing from Preston. *[David Hocquard/Roy Fenton collection]*

Kenrix (3) as built. *[Company archives]*

Kenrix (3) on 24th August 1977 after lengthening. *[Michael Green}*

1993: Sold to Mohamad Abdelrazak Yamak and Co., Tartous, Syria and renamed AL HAJEH MARIAM.
1995: Sold to Syrian flag operators and renamed EMAN.
6.2011: Deleted by 'Lloyd's Register' as continued existence in doubt.

36. FYLRIX 1962-1984
O.N. 301691 IMO 5185257 598g 366n 830d
188.7 x 28.2 x 11.7 feet
1967: 637g 418n 930d
203.1 x 28.2 x 11.7 feet
2SCSA 8-cyl. oil engine by Appingedammer Bronsmoterenfabriek, Appingedam, Netherlands; 660 BHP, 10.5 knots.
31.3.1962: Launched by v/h A. Apol C.V. Scheepswerf 'Appingedam', Appingedam (Yard No. 191) for J.R. Rix and Sons Ltd., Hull, as FYLRIX.
5.1962: Completed
1967: Lengthened.
1984: Transferred to Highseas Ltd. (J.R. Rix and Sons Ltd, managers), Hull.
21.11.1984: Cargo of granite chippings shifted in severe weather approximately 10 miles off the Eddystone Lighthouse while on a voyage from Dean Quarry to London.
22.11.1984: Sank at 3.00 am in Jennycliff Bay, Plymouth Sound. Three of her crew of seven were lifted off by naval helicopter while her master and remaining crew were rescued by the Plymouth Lifeboat. Declared a constructive total loss and abandoned to P.R. Eurosalve Ltd., Folkestone for salvage.

37. WHITEHAVEN/LESRIX (3) 1964-1986
O.N. 186872 IMO 5389011
676g 376n 950d
185.0 x 32.7 x 12.0 feet
9.1971: 726g 436n 1,000d
200.7 x 32.7 x 12.0 feet
4SCSA 6-cyl. oil engine by Klockner-Humboldt-Deutz A.G., Köln-Deutz, West Germany; 755 BHP, 11 knots.
9.10.1957: Launched by Jos. L. Meyer Schiffswerft, Papenburg a.d. Ems, West Germany (Yard No.485) for the Whitehaven Shipping Co. Ltd., Grimsby (Anthony and Bainbridge Ltd., Newcastle-upon-Tyne, managers) as WHITEHAVEN.
11.1957: Completed.
1964: Company and vessel acquired by J.R. Rix and Sons Ltd., Hull and renamed LESRIX.
9.1971: Lengthened.
1977: Transferred to J.R. Rix and Sons Ltd., Hull.
1981: Transferred to Whitehaven Shipping Co. Ltd. (J.R. Rix and Sons Ltd., managers), Hull.
1986: Sold to Jellwing Ltd., Sittingbourne, renamed NAN 1 and registered in Honduras.
14.10.1987: Laid up at Rochester.
12.9.1990: Arrived at Zeebrugge in tow of St. Vincent-registered tug TOWING CHIEFTAN (168/1963) having been sold to Brugse Scheepssloperij, Bruges, Belgium.
1992: Resold, renamed CHADA and remaining registered in Honduras.

Fylrix at a South Wales port. *[J. and M. Clarkson collection]*

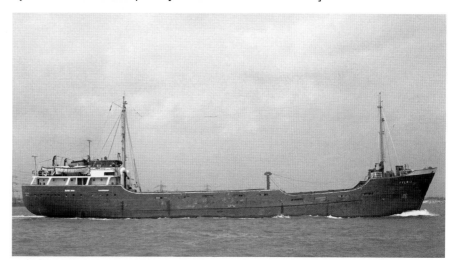
The lengthened *Fylrix* sailing from the Thames on 10th July 1975. *[J. and M. Clarkson]*

Whitehaven in Whitehaven Shipping funnel colours. *[World Ship Society Ltd.]*

Lesrix (3) after lengthening. *[FotoFlite incorporating Skyfotos]*

1993: Sold to Mohammad Mustafa Al Shaman, Tartous, Syria and renamed SHAMAN 1.
1994: Sold to Mustafa Abdulla Sabra, Tartous, Syria and renamed UROUBA 1.
4.3.2004: Arrived at Constanta, Roumania to be broken up.

38. TIMRIX (1) 1972-1975
O.N. 342734   IMO 7204469   499g 334n
193.5 x 32.5 x 11.5 feet
4SCSA 6-cyl. oil engine by Motorenwerke Mannheim A.G., Mannheim, West Germany; 800 BHP, 11 knots.

16.9.1965: Launched by Martin Jansen Schiffswerft, Leer, West Germany (Yard No. 75).
1965: Completed for Alois Held, Haren-Ems, West Germany as MAJO.
1972: Acquired by J.R. Rix and Sons Ltd., Hull and renamed TIMRIX.

Timrix (1). *[FotoFlite incorporating Skyfotos]*

1975: Sold to Sugar Maritime (Union Transport (London) Ltd., managers), London, renamed UNION CRYSTAL and registered in Singapore.
1977: Transferred to Jencar Ltd. (Union Transport (London) Ltd., managers), London retaining Singapore registry.
16.11.1977: Sank in a position 50.27 north, 05.34 west after developing a severe list in a storm while on a voyage from Kilroot to Poole with a cargo of rock salt. Her crew of six had abandoned her 12 miles north of Cape Cornwall but only her master survived.

39. SALRIX (1) 1974-1992

O.N. 362214 IMO 6519479 598g 295n 195d
65.23 x 9.81 x 4.014 metres.
4SCSA 8-cyl. oil engine by Klockner-Humboldt-Deutz A.G., Köln-Deutz, West Germany.
23.7.1965: Launched by Jac. Bodewes Scheepsbouwwerf 'Hoogezand', Hoogezand, Netherlands (Yard No. 129) for Greenore Ferry Services Ltd., Dublin (Limerick Steamship Co.

Ltd., Limerick, managers) as OWENRO.
10.1965: Completed.
1968: Management ceased.
1974: Acquired by Rix Shipping Co. Ltd. (J.R. Rix and Sons Ltd., managers), Hull and renamed SALRIX.
1987: Transferred to the Salrix Shipping Co. Ltd. (Rix Shipping Co. Ltd., managers), Hull.
1992: Registered in the Bahamas.
1992: Sold to Ali Fal and Co. (General Trading and Shipping Co., managers), Tartous, Syria, and renamed ABDOULLAH S, later amended to ABDOULLAH F.
1996: Sold to Hussein Moustafa Yamak and Co., Tartous and renamed AL FADEL LELAH.
1999: Sold to Mohamad Mustafa Jawhar and Co. (Bashar Shipping, managers), Tartous and renamed WAEL II.
7.5.2001: Sank 53 miles south east of Crete in position 34.34 north, 27.17 east after her cargo of cement shifted in rough weather while on a voyage from Alexandria to Kiato, Greece. Her crew of eight was rescued.

40. IRISHGATE/JEMRIX 1974-1994

O.N. 305788 IMO 6512342 800g 441n 950d
61.17 x 9.83 x 3.658 metres
1986: 843g 465n 1,250d
71.53 x 9.83 x 4.141 metres
Two 4SCSA 8-cyl. oil engines by Blackstone and Co. Ltd., Stamford single reduction-geared to a single screw shaft; 1,320 BHP.
31.3.1965: Launched by Cleland's Shipbuilding Co. Ltd., Wallsend-on-Tyne (Yard No. 278) for Hull Gates Shipping Co. Ltd. (S.F. Craggs and Co. Ltd., managers), Hull as IRISHGATE.
5.1965: Completed.
1974: Acquired by J.R. Rix and Sons Ltd., Hull.
1974: Renamed JEMRIX.
1984: Transferred to Highseas Ltd. (J.R. Rix and Sons Ltd., managers), Hull.
1985: Transferred to the Jemrix Shipping Co. Ltd. (J.R. Rix and Sons Ltd., managers), Hull.
1986: Lengthened.
1987: Managers became Rix Shipping Co. Ltd., Hull.

Salrix (1) at sea on 8th May 1990. *[FotoFlite incorporating SkyFotos, 96792]*

The former *Salrix* (1) sinking as *Wael II* in May 2001 *[Company archives]*

1989: Registered in the Bahamas.
1994: Sold to Scania Navigation Corporation, Panama (S.J.H. Marine Ltd., Crediton, Devon).
1995: Sold to Naviera Kathleen Shipping S. de R.L., Belize, renamed KATHLEEN D and registered in Honduras.
12.1995: Detained by the US Coast Guard at Mobile, Alabama on arrival from Isla De San Andres because of safety and structural defects.
7.1.1996: Foundered approximately 180 miles from Mobile after she capsized when her stern was submerged by a wave. One of her crew was rescued by the US-flag MARINE DUVAL (11,080/44). She had sailed the previous day from Mobile with a cargo of hydrated lime and eight deck containers having met minimum SOLAS safety standards.

41. TIMRIX (2) 1984-1995
O.N. 343137 IMO 7204409
783g 448n 1,180d
61.73 x 10.47 x 3.937 metres
1978: 954g 594n 1,393d
72.73 x 10.47 x 3.763 metres
4SCSA 8-cyl. oil engine by W.H. Allen, Sons and Co. Ltd., Bedford; 1,160 BHP, 12 knots.
2.2.1972: Launched by Cochrane and Sons Ltd., Selby (Yard No. 1542) for Metcalf Motor Coasters Ltd. (Tertius Metcalf, manager), London as NELLIE M.
4.1972: Completed.
1973: Managers became S. William Coe and Co. Ltd., Liverpool.
1978: Transferred to Coe Metcalf Shipping Ltd., Liverpool and lengthened.
7.2.1981: While moored off Moville, in Lough Foyle during a voyage from Blyth to Coleraine with 1,260 tons of coal, boarded by seven masked men who had hijacked the Moville pilot boat, forcing the pilot to take them out to the vessel. Once on board they planted three bombs and forced the nine crew on to the pilot boat and then into a rubber dinghy which was towed toward the shore. Only one bomb exploded, causing the vessel to sink in Irish Republic waters. The Provisional IRA claimed responsibility for the attack as the vessel was a commercial target. Irish bomb disposal experts subsequently cleared the partly submerged vessel of explosives. Abandoned as a constructive total loss to her underwriters, the wreck was sold to P.R. Eurosalve Ltd., Folkestone.
12.7.1981: Refloated and subsequently towed to Londonderry where she was discharged and later repaired.
1982: Sold to Lofoten Compania Naviera, Panama and renamed ELLIE.
1984: Sold to Phoenix Offshore Ltd., Wadebridge retaining Panama registry.
1984: Acquired by the Timrix Shipping Co. Ltd. (J.R. Rix and Sons Ltd., managers), Hull and renamed TIMRIX.
1987: Managers became Rix Shipping Co. Ltd., Hull.
1991: Registered in the Bahamas.

Jemrix as built (top) and after lengthening (middle). *[Roy Cressey; FotoFlite incorporating Skyfotos, 71472]*

Timrix (2) as the *Ellie* soon after her arrival at Paull shipyard. *[Company archives]*

1995: Sold to Apex Maritime Ltd., Malta (Seaflight Ltd., London, managers) and renamed MALTESE VENTURE.
1996: Sold to Modern Marine Operations, St. Helier, Jersey (Pro Chart B.V., Rotterdam, Netherlands, managers) and renamed SPEZI, retaining Malta registry.
1997: Sold to Simon Lyon-Smith and others, Crediton, Devon.
1997: Sold to Maritima Santa Catalina, Isla de San Andres, Columbia.
1998: Sold to Caribbean Island Shipping

Timrix (2) underway in the English Channel after having the coamings at number 2 hatch raised to increase her capacity for lightweight cargoes such as animal feeds. *[FotoFlite incorporating Skyfotos, 154965]*

Inc., Isla de Providencia, Colombia and renamed DOVE under the Belize flag.
2000: Sold to St. Marten Ltda., Cartagena de Indias, Colombia.
2003: Renamed AMAZON'S DOLPHIN.
5.2009: Sold and renamed OCEANIC LADY under the St. Vincent and Grenadines flag
3.2011: Renamed CARMEN II under the flag of Sao Thome and Principe.
2.2014: Still listed by 'Lloyd's Register'.

42. ROBRIX (4) 1985-1995
O.N. 338115 IMO 7392244 798g 504n 1,184d
61.73 x 10.47 x 3.937 metres
4SCSA 8-cyl. oil engine by W.H. Allen, Sons and Co. Ltd., Bedford; 1,201 BHP.
31.12.1973: Launched by Beverley Shipbuilding and Engineering Co. Ltd., Beverley (Yard No. 1562) for Tilstone Construction Co. Ltd., London as TILSTONE MAID.
3.1974: Completed but not registered.
10.4.1974: Sold to Stag Line Ltd., North Shields for £585,412, including minor modifications, and renamed SILLOTH STAG.
21.4.1974: Bareboat chartered to Silloth Shipping, Annan.
27.5.1982: Redelivered, managers became G.T. Gillie and Blair Ltd, North Shields.
1.7.1982: Sold to Westfield Shipping Co. Ltd. (G.T. Gillie and Blair Ltd., managers). North Shields.
1983: Managers became Hunting Stag Shipmanagement Ltd., Newcastle-upon-Tyne.
1985: Sold to Coe Metcalf Ltd., Liverpool.
1985: Acquired by Rix Shipping Co. Ltd. (J.R. Rix and Sons Ltd., managers), Hull and renamed ROBRIX.
1987: Transferred to Robrix Shipping Co.

Two views of *Robrix* (4). *[Company archives; FotoFlite incorporating Skyfotos]*

Two views of *Magrix* (3). *[FotoFlite incorporating Skyfotos, 207941; Michael Green]*

Ltd. (Rix Shipping Co. Ltd., managers), Hull.
1994: Registered in the Bahamas.
1995: Sold to Aned Maritime Ltd., Malta
(Seaflight Management Consultants,
London, managers) and renamed SPRITE.
1997: Managers became Pro Chart B.V.,
Ridderkerk, Netherlands.
1997: Sold to Nortrans Shipping Group Inc.,
Limasol, Cyprus, renamed KONVIK and
registered in Belize.
1998: Sold to Edarte ShPK Import Export,
Durres, Albania, renamed EDARTE and
remaining registered in Belize.
2002: Transferred to Frojdi ShPK Shipping
and Trading (Vital Shipping Co., managers),
Durres and renamed FROJDI I.
2004: Transferred to Edarte ShPK Import
Export, Durres.
2005: Transferred to Alb Sea Transport
ShPK (Vital Shipping Co., managers),
Durres.
2.2014: Still listed by 'Lloyd's Register'.

43. MAGRIX (3) 1987-1998

O.N. 712664 IMO 7529328
938g 600n 1,559d
65.82 x 10.80 x 4.292 metres
1987: 998g 699n 1,898d
78.44 x 10.80 x 4.292 metres
4SCSA 16-cyl. Vee-type oil engine by
Caterpillar Tractor Co., Peoria, Illinois,
USA; 1,006 BHP.
7.3.1976: Launched by Scheepswerf &
Machinefabriek Barkmeijer Stroobos B.V.,
Stroobos, Netherlands (Yard No. 204)
for H.P. Holwerda (Scheepvaartkantoor
Holwerda, managers), Heerenveen,
Netherlands as ROELOF HOLWERDA.
11.6.1976: Completed.
1980: Transferred to Rederij H. and P.

Holwerda (Scheepvaartkantoor Holwerda,
managers), Heerenveen.
1981: Transferred to Rederij Roelof
Holwerda, Heerenveen and renamed TANJA
HOLWERDA.
1984: Managers became Holwerda
Scheepvaartkantoor B.V., Heerenveen.
1987: Transferred to Rederij H. and P.
Holwerda (Holwerda Scheepvaartkantoor
B.V., managers), Heerenveen.
1987: Transferred to Bluearrow Ltd., Cyprus
(Holwerda Scheepvaartkantoor B.V.,
Heerenveen, managers) and renamed THE
DUTCH.
27.7.1987: Developed a list and severely
flooded after her deck cargo of timber
shifted in a position 54.33 north by 01.25
east while on a voyage from Archangel to
Boston, Lincolnshire. The list was reduced
after some cargo was jettisoned.

29.7.1987: Arrived at Hull in tow of the tug
SEAMAN (499/1985) and after inspection
of her engine room and accommodation was
declared a constructive total loss.
15.9.1987: Sold to Humber Tugs Ltd.,
Immingham.
1987: Acquired by The Magrix Shipping
Co. Ltd. (Rix Shipping Co. Ltd., managers),
Hull, repaired, lengthened and renamed
MAGRIX.
1998: Sold to Waveney Shipping II plc,
Great Yarmouth (R. Lapthorn and Co. Ltd.,
Rochester, managers) and renamed NICKY L.
1999: Sold to S.J.H. Marine Group,
Crediton, Devon.
1999: Sold to Med Express Inc., Panama
(Dick Van der Kamp Shipsales B.V.,
Hellevoetsluis, Netherlands, managers).
24.3.1999: Arrived at Rotterdam to lay up
pending sale.

Jonrix (2) in heavy weather (above) and below in calmer waters in her home port of Hull. *[FotoFlite incorporating Skyfotos, 296583; Patrick Hill/George Robinson]*

7.1999: Sold to Abalone Shipping Services S.A., Panama (Mainport Marine Services, Schiedam, Netherlands, managers), renamed ABALONE and registered in Belize.
3.3.2004: Towed into Georgetown, Cayman Islands with severe engine damage.
6.5.2004: Arrived under tow at Belize City where part of her steel cargo was discharged. She was then to be towed to Tampico to complete discharge.
2004: Registered in Mexico.
2.2014: Still listed by 'Lloyd's Register'.

44. JONRIX (2) 1994-2007
IMO 7530846 999g 671n 2,210d
79.00 x 12.45 x 4.776 metres
4SCSA 6-cyl. oil engine by Yanmar Diesel Engine Co. Ltd., Amagasaki, Japan; 1,600 BHP, 11.5 knots.
24.9.1976: Launched by Kyokuyo Zosen Tekkosho, Hikoshima, Japan (Yard No. 501) for Partenreederei m.s. Langeland (Gunther Schulz Schulauer Schiffahrtskontor, managers), Hamburg, West Germany as LANGELAND.
2.1977: Completed.
1983: Renamed LANGELAND II.
1983: Managers became Antarktis und Spezialfahrt Schiffahrtsgesellschaft m.b.H., Wedel, West Germany.
1988: Managers became Reiseburo Luhrs K.G., Hamburg.
1992: Managers became Aug. Bolten Wm. Muller's Nachfolger, Hamburg and registered in Antigua and Barbuda.
1994: Acquired by The Jonrix Shipping Co. Ltd. (Rix Shipping Co. Ltd., managers), Hull, renamed JONRIX and registered in the Bahamas.
2002: Registered in the United Kingdom.

2007: Sold to Orrisdale Shipping Ltd., Isle of Man (Millwood Shipping Inc., London, managers; D. and H. Freight Management Ltd., Newent, chartering agents) and renamed JONSEN.
3.2012: Broken up at Aliaga, Turkey by Demtas Denizcilik Turizm Sanay.

45. BREYDON VENTURE/RIX HAWK 1995-2013 Black oil tanker
IMO 7533630 562g 321n 1,036d
45.93 x 9.96 x 3.88 metres
4SCSA 6-cyl. oil engine by Caterpillar Tractor Co., Peoria, Illinois, USA; 710 NHP, 9.75 knots.
11.1998: Two 4SCSA 8-cyl. oil engines by Caterpillar Tractor Co., Peoria, Illinois, USA; 479 BHP.
25.8.1976: Launched by Yorkshire Dry Dock

Co. Ltd., Hull (Yard No. 241) for Eggar Forrester (Holdings) Ltd., London (R. Lapthorn and Co. Ltd., Rochester, managers) as WIS.
1.1977: Completed.
2.1985: Managers became Wilks Shipping Co. Ltd., London.
6.1985: Managers became F.T. Everard and Sons Management Ltd., London.
6.1986: Sold to Breydon Marine Ltd, Great Yarmouth and renamed BREYDON VENTURE.
1992: Managers became Genchem Marine Ltd., Ipswich.
1995: Acquired by Jemrix Shipping Co. Ltd. (Rix Shipping Co. Ltd., managers), Hull.
15.12.1997: Laid up.
23.7.1999: Transferred to Rix Hawk Shipping Co. Ltd. (Rix Shipping Co. Ltd., managers), Hull following conversion to a

bunkering tanker, and renamed RIX HAWK.
3.3.2003: Transferred to Rix Tankships Ltd.
(Rix Shipping Co. Ltd., managers), Hull.
2.4.2003: Transferred to The Rix Hawk
Tankship Ltd. (Rix Shipping Co. Ltd.,
managers), Hull.
2009: Registered in Roumania for the
duration of a two-year bunkering contract to
the Roumanian state oil company.
3.2011: Registered in the Isle of Man.
2.2013: Sold to Skyshore Shipping and
Energy Ltd., Port Harcourt, Nigeria and
renamed RESTORER II.
2.2014: Still listed by 'Lloyd's Register'.

46. BREYDON ENTERPRISE/RIX HARRIER 1995- Black oil tanker
IMO 7802093 572g 354n 1,046d
45.73 x 9.50 x 3.879 metres
Two 4SCSA 4-cyl. oil engines by Caterpillar
Tractor Co., Peoria, Illinois, USA.
1.1997: Two 4SCSA 4-cyl. oil engines by
Caterpillar Tractor Co., Peoria, Illinois,
USA; 479 BHP, 8.5 knots.
16.10.1978: Launched by Yorkshire Dry
Dock Co. Ltd., Hull (Yard No. 257) for Eggar
Forrester (Holdings) Ltd., London (R. Lapthorn
and Co. Ltd., Rochester, managers) as WIB.
5.2.1979: Completed.
2.1985: Managers became Wilks Shipping
Co. Ltd.
10.1985: Managers became F.T. Everard and
Sons Management Ltd., London.
6.1986: Sold to Breydon Marine Ltd., Great
Yarmouth.
3.1987: Renamed BREYDON ENTERPRISE.
1992: Managers became Genchem Marine
Ltd., Ipswich.
10.1995: Acquired by T. and S. Rix Ltd. (Rix
Shipping Co. Ltd., managers), Hull.
1.1997: Completed conversion to a
bunkering tanker, fitted with a new engine
and renamed RIX HARRIER
23.7.1999: Transferred to The Rix Harrier
Shipping Co. Ltd. (Rix Shipping Co. Ltd.,
managers), Hull.
3.3.2003: Transferred to Rix Tankships Ltd.
(Rix Shipping Co. Ltd., managers), Hull.
2.4.2003: Transferred to The Rix Harrier
Tankship Ltd. (Rix Shipping Co. Ltd.,
managers), Hull.
10.2010: Registered in the Isle of Man.
2.2014: In the current fleet.

47. LIZRIX (1) 1995-2002
IMO 7624336 2,019g 913n 3,050d
82.30 x 13.90 x 5.30 metres
4SCSA 6-cyl. oil engine by Motorenwerke
Mannheim A.G., Mannheim, West Germany;
2,600 BHP, 11.5 knots.
6.8.1977: Launched by Scheepswerf
'Friesland' N.V., Lemmer, Netherlands
(Yard No. 365) for Intersee, Rotterdam,
Netherlands as ERIESEE.
5.10.1977: Completed.
1978: Sold to Noordlijn B.V., later
Scheepsbedrift Nordlijn, Emmen,
Netherlands and renamed KARLSVIK.
1979: Managers became Intersee Schiffahrts
G.m.b.H. and Co. K.G., Haren-Ems, West

The dry cargo *Breydon Venture* was converted to a tanker and renamed *Rix Hawk* (above*). [Roy Cressey]*

Breydon Enterprise (middle) was also converted to a tanker and as *Rix Harrier* is seen on 15th February 1997 (bottom). *[Roy Cressey; Michael Green]*

Germany.

1983: Management ceased.

1986: Sold to Katharina Shipping Co.
Ltd., Cyprus (NORA Reederi und
Verwaltungesellschaft m.b.H., Haren-
Ems, West Germany, managers) and
renamed KATHARINA.

1990: Transferred to Trush Shipping Co.
Ltd., Nicosia, Cyprus (NORA Reederi
und Verwaltungsellschaft m.b.H.,
Haren-Ems, managers) and renamed
YORKSEE.

13.12.1995: Acquired by Lizrix Shipping
Co. Ltd. (Rix Shipping Co Ltd.,
managers), Hull, renamed LIZRIX and
registered in the Bahamas.

7.2.2002: Sold to Aquarius Navigation
Ltd., Malta (Alpha Shipping Agency,
Riga, Latvia, managers), renamed
AIVITA remaining registered in the
Bahamas.

2002: Managers became Duglas Ltd., St.
Petersburg, Russia and registered in St.
Vincent and the Grenadines.

2009: Managers became Alpha Shipping
Co. SIA, Riga.

1.2011: Broken up.

Lizrix (1). *[FotoFlite incorporating Skyfotos, 296583]*

48. HARRIX 1998-2010

IMO 7530884 1,992g 1,120n 2,750d
79.10 x 12.43 x 5.422 metres
4SCSA 6-cyl. oil engine by Yanmar
Diesel Engine Co. Ltd., Amagasaki,
Japan; 1,600 BHP, 10.5 knots.

25.10.1976: Launched by Hashimoto
Zosensho, Hinase, Japan (Yard No.
500) for Peter Deilman, Neustadt, West
Germany as NORDHOLM.

15.12.1976: Completed.

1977: Transferred to Partenreederei
'Nordholm' (Peter Deilman, managers),
Neustadt.

1979: Sold to Schiffahrts K.G.
Beteilgungsgesellschaft Alster m.b.H.
and Co. (Edmund Halm and Co.
G.m.b.H,. managers), Hamburg,
West Germany and renamed
BARKENKOPPEL.

1986: Sold to Bulkcarrier Schiffahrtsges.
m.b.H. & Co. K.G. (Osterreichischer
Lloyd Bereederungsgesellschaft m.b.H.,
managers), Vienna, Austria and renamed
BETTINA.

1989: Managers became Osterreichischer
Lloyd/Krohn Shipping Group, Vienna.

1990: Transferred to m.s. 'Stuben'
Osterreichischer Lloyd G.m.b.H. and
Co. K.G. (Osterreichischer Lloyd/Krohn
Shipmanagement G.m.b.H., managers),
Vienna.

1994: Transferred to Geschwister Krohn
Schiffahrtsgesellschaft m.b.H. Co. K.G.
(Osterreichischer Lloyd Shipmanagement
G.m.b.H., managers), Vienna.

14.1.1998: Acquired by The Harrix
Shipping Co. Ltd. (Rix Shipping Co.
Ltd., managers), Hull, renamed HARRIX
and registered in the Bahamas.

2002: Registered in the United Kingdom.

3.2010: Sold to Mantic Marine Co.,

Harrix discharging packaged timber at Hull. *[Company archives]*

Harrix dry docked at Hull on 24th September 1999. *[Michael Green]*

Lerrix (1) in the Kiel Canal. *[Company archives]*

Marshall Islands, renamed HARMONIA and
registered in Moldova.
9.2.2011: Arrived at Aliaga to be broken up
by Shirdi Steel Traders.
16.2.2011: Work began.

49. LERRIX (1) 1998-2010
IMO 7530901 1,992g 1,143n 2,777d
79.13 x 12.43 x 5.422 metres
4SCSA 6-cyl. oil engine by Yanmar Diesel
Engine Co. Ltd., Amagasaki, Japan; 1,600
BHP, 10.5 knots.
9.2.1977: Launched by Rinkai Kogyo K.K.,
Setoda, Japan (Yard No. 32) for Reederei
m.s. 'Sanderskoppel', West Germany as
SANDERSKOPPEL.
6.1977: Completed for Schiffahrts K.G.
Beteilgungsgesellschaft Alster m.b.H. & Co.,
Hamburg, West Germany.
1977: Managers became Edmund Halm & Co.
G.m.b.H., Hamburg.
1986: Sold to Bulkcarrier
Schiffahrtsgesellschaft m.b.H. &
Co. K.G. (Osterreichischer Lloyd
Bereederungsgesellschaft m.b.H., managers),
Vienna, Austria and renamed STEFAN.
1989: Managers became Osterreichischer
Lloyd/Krohn Shipping Group, Vienna.
1992: Transferred to m.s. 'Stuben'
Osterreichischer Lloyd G.m.b.H. & Co. K.G.
(Osterreichischer Lloyd Shipmanagement
G.m.b.H., managers), Vienna.
1994: Transferred to Geschwister Krohn
Schiffahrtsgesellschaft m.b.H. Co. K.G.
(Osterreichischer Lloyd Shipmanagement
G.m.b.H., managers), Vienna.
21.1.1998: Acquired by The Lerrix Shipping
Co. Ltd. (Rix Shipping Co. Ltd., managers),

Hull, renamed LERRIX and registered in the
Bahamas.
2002: Registered in the United Kingdom.
3.2010: Sold to Anawan Navigation Co.,
Marshall Islands, renamed LEON and
registered in Moldova.
21.6.2011: Arrived at Aliaga, Turkey to be
broken up by Sok Denizcilik Tic Ltd. Sti.

50. TIMRIX (3) 1998-2003
IMO 7525607 1,973g 853n 2,206d
78.97 x 12.43 x 4.771 metres
4SCSA 6-cyl. oil engine by Yanmar Diesel
Engine Co. Ltd., Amagasaki, Japan; 1,600
BHP, 12 knots.
5.2.1977: Launched by Imamura

Zosen, Kure, Japan (Yard No. 213) for
Schiffahrtsgesellschaft K.G. 'Siggen' m.b.h.
(Edmund Halm & Co. G.m.b.h., managers),
Hamburg, West Germany as SIGGEN.
18.7.1977: Completed.
1985: Managers became Gunther Schulz
Schulauer Schiffahrtskontor, Wedel, West
Germany and renamed SIGGEN II.
1986: Managers became Antarktis und
Spezialfahrt Schiffahrtsgesellschaft m.b.H.,
Wedel and registered in Panama.
1987: Managers became Saturn Bereederungs-
und Befrachtungsgesellschaft m.b.H., Wedel.
1988: Transferred to Partenreederei m.s.
'Siggen II' (Saturn Bereederungs-und
Befrachtungsgesellschaft m.b.H., managers),

Timrix (3) arriving Hull with containers (opposite page, bottom) and discharging timber at Hull on 26th May 2001 (above).
[Company archives; Michael Green]

Wedel and registered in Antigua and Barbuda.
1994: Registered in Tuvalu.
20.5.1997: Two crew members injured when a fire broke out in the engine room while waiting to sail from Shoreham with scrap. Vessel was arrested by the Maritime Safety Agency the following day.
1997: Sold to Ronel Shipping Inc., Panama (Alexanders Partners (Shipbroking) Ltd., Ilford, managers), renamed KIRI and registered in Barbados.
1999: Acquired by Timrix Shipping Co. Ltd. (Rix Shipping Co. Ltd., managers), Hull, renamed TIMRIX and registered in the Bahamas.
2002: Registered in the United Kingdom.
2003: Sold to Leena Shipping N.V., Netherlands Antilles (Troy Shipping Ltd., Istanbul, Turkey, managers), renamed TEOS.
2006: Registered in the Dominican Republic.
2007: Sold to Dava International Shipping, Netherlands Antilles (Erk Shipping and Trading Co. Ltd. (Erk Denizcilik ve Tic Ltd.), Sti, Istanbul, managers), renamed AYSENUR and remaining registered in the Dominican Republic.
6.2010: Registered in Moldova.
2.2014: Still listed by 'Lloyd's Register'.

51. RIX CONDOR 1999-2008 Black oil tanker

IMO 6722284 500g 330n 1,153d
64.74 x 9.83 x 3.80 metres
1981: 827g 425n 1,240d
72.85 x 9.83 x 3.703 metres
4SCSA 6-cyl. oil engine by Motorenwerke Mannheim A.G., Mannheim, West Germany; 810 BHP.
8.1974: 4SCSA 8-cyl. oil engine by Motorenwerke Mannheim A.G., Mannheim,

Rix Condor on 16th March 2007. *[Michael Green]*

West Germany.
19.3.1967: Launched by Krögerwerf G.m.b.H. & Co. K.G., Rendsburg, West Germany (Yard No. 1345) for Tankskibrederi Herning (Peder G.K. Lysgaard, manager), Herning, Denmark as GRETE THERESA.
8.1967: Completed.
1969: Manager became Fru V.T. Lysgaard, Herning until 1972.
1975: Transferred to Tankskibsrederiet Herning I/S, Herning.
1981: Lengthened.
1989: Registered in the Faeroe Islands.
1990: Sold to K/S Silja (Alba Shipping Ltd. A/S, managers), Aalborg, Denmark, renamed SILJA and registered in Panama.
12.1993: Sold to Azteca 90 II (Guernsey) Ltd., St. Peter Port, Guernsey (Camper and Nicholsons International Ltd., Monte Carlo,

managers), renamed ECO SUPPORTER and retaining Panama registry.
9.1999: Acquired by T and S. Rix Ltd. (Rix Shipping Co. Ltd., managers), Hull, having being laid up at Hull due to overdue surveys. On completion of surveys renamed RIX CONDOR.
5.2000: Transferred to Rix Condor Ltd. (Rix Shipping Co. Ltd., managers), Hull.
3.2003: Transferred to The Rix Condor Tankship Ltd. (Rix Shipping Co. Ltd., managers), Hull.
11.2008: Sold to Woodham Enterprise Ltd., London, renamed OKIKI and registered in Comoros.
7.5.2013: Caught fire 135 miles south west of Port Harcourt, Nigeria in position 03.10 north, 05.55 east. The crew of 13 abandoned the vessel and were rescued.

52. SALRIX (2) 2002-2012

IMO 7530858 2,563g 1,174n 2,908d
96.32 (inc BB) x 12.43 x 4.728 metres
4SCSA 6-cyl. oil engine by Yanmar Diesel
Engine Co. Ltd., Amagasaki, Japan; 1,600
BHP, 10.5 knots
10.1.1977: Launched by Kyokuyo Zosen
Tekko K.K., Hikoshima, Japan (Yard No.
502) for Securitas Compania Naviera,
Panama (Horst Bartels, Hamburg, West
Germany, managers) as NEUKLOSTER.
12.1977: Completed by Hyundai Mipo
Dockyard Co. Ltd., Ulsan, South Korea (Yard
No. 2563) after lengthening by 16.8 metres.
1981: Sold to Schulauer Schiffscharter
G.m.b.H. & Co. K.G. (Gunther Schultz
Schulauer Schiffahrtskontor, managers),
Wedel, West Germany and renamed
BORNHOLM.
1986: Sold to m.s. Bregenz
Schiffahrtsgesellschaft m.b.H. & Co. K.G.,
Vienna, Austria (Edmund Halm & Co.
G.m.b.H., Hamburg, managers) and renamed
BREGENZ.
1992: Sold to Bulkship (Overseas) Ltd.,
Cyprus (Fisser & van Doornum, Hamburg,
managers) and renamed BORSSUM.
1995: Sold to Emerald Isle Bulkers Ltd., Cork,
Irish Republic (K.G. Fisser & van Doornum
G.m.b.H. & Co., Hamburg, West Germany,
managers) and renamed KYLEMORE.
1998: Managers became Edmund Halm and
Co. G.m.b.H., Hamburg.
5.2001: Registered in Antigua and Barbuda.
4.2002: Acquired by Salrix Shipping Co.
Ltd. (Rix Shipping Co Ltd., managers), Hull
and renamed SALRIX.
10.2007: Transferred to Ronrix Shipping Co.
Ltd. (Rix Shipping Co Ltd., managers), Hull.
1.2009: Transferred to Salrix Shipping Co.
Ltd. (Rix Shipping Co Ltd., managers), Hull
4.2012: Sold to Southern Seaways Ltd.,
Marshall Islands (Pasifik Logistik Grubu ve
Denizcilik A.S., Istanbul, Turkey), renamed
GULF SOUTH and registered in St Kitts
Nevis.
12.2013: Registered in Togo.
30.12.2013: Arrived at Aliaga, Turkey to be
broken up.

53. RONRIX 2002-2012

IMO 7530872 2,501g 1,132n 2,908d
96.25 (inc BB) x 12.43 x 4.771 metres
4SCSA 6-cyl. oil engine by Yanmar Diesel
Engine Co. Ltd., Amagasaki, Japan; 1,600
BHP, 12 knots.
8.7.1977: Launched by Kyokuyo Zosen
Tekko K.K., Hiroshima, Japan (Yard No. 504)
for Peter Dohle Schiffahrts K.G., Hamburg,
West Germany as NEUWULMSTORF.
12.1977: Completed by Hyundai Mipo
Dockyard Co. Ltd., Ulsan, South Korea (Yard
No. 1289), after lengthening by 16.8 metres.
1981: Sold to Partenreederei m.s. 'Anholt'
(Edmund Halm & Co. G.m.b.H., managers),
Hamburg and renamed ANHOLT.
1986: Sold to Athlacca Ltd., Cork, Irish
Republic (Fisser & van Doornum, Hamburg,
managers) and renamed KILLARNEY.
1991: Sold to Emerald Isle Bulkers Ltd.,

Salrix (2) on 31st May 2003. *[Michael Green]*

Ronrix. [FotoFlite incorporating Skyfotos, 352296]

Cork (Edmund Halm & Co. G.m.b.H.,
Hamburg, managers).
1993: Managers became Fisser & van
Doornum G.m.b.H. & Co., Hamburg.
1998: Managers became Edmund Halm &
Co. G.m.b.H., Hamburg.
2001: Registered in Antigua and Barbuda.
6.2002: Acquired by Ronrix Shipping Co.
Ltd. (Rix Shipping Co. Ltd., managers), Hull
and renamed RONRIX.
4.2012: Sold to Southern Seaways Ltd.,
Marshall Islands (Pasifik Logistik Grubu ve
Denizcilik A.S., Istanbul, Turkey), renamed
GULF NORTH and registered in St Kitts
Nevis.
5.9.2013: Arrived at Aliaga, Turkey to be
broken up by Aliaga Gemi Geri Donusum.

54. ROBRIX (5) 2004-2005

IMO 9019573 2,364g 1,321n 2,685d
82.4 (inc BB) x 12.8 x 5.768 metres
2SCSA 6-cyl. oil engine by Wartsila-
Wichman Diesel A.S., Rubbestadneset,
Norway; 2,447 BHP, 12.5 knots.
16.11.1990: Launched by Van Mill B.V.,
Hardinxveld-Giessendam, Netherlands (Yard
No. 164) for Reedererei Jurgen Speck K.G.,
Breiholz, Germany (Christian Jurgensen,

Brink & Wolffel Schiffahrts G.m.b.H. &
Co., Flensburg, Germany, managers) as
NORDIC BRIDGE.
2.1991: Completed.
1991: Renamed ULLA.
1992: Transferred to Speck Schiffahrts
G.m.b.H. & Co. K.G. (Christian Jurgensen,
Brink & Wolffel Schiffahrts G.m.b.H. &
Co., managers) Flensburg and registered in
Antigua and Barbuda.
1993: Sold to Katharina Shipping Co. Ltd.,
Antigua and Barbuda (Osterreichischer
Lloyd Shipmanagement G.m.b.H., Vienna,
Austria, managers) and renamed AMOR.
1993: Renamed WERFEN.
1994: Transferred to W. Krohn Schiffahrts
G.m.b.H. & Co. K.G. (Osterreichischer
Lloyd Shipmanagement G.m.b.H.,
managers), Vienna.
2001: Sold to Rederij K. & T. Holland C.V.
(Flagship Management Co. B.V., managers),
Farmsum, Netherlands.
3.2004: Acquired by Robrix Shipping Co.
Ltd. (Rix Shipping Co. Ltd., managers), Hull
and renamed ROBRIX.
11.2005: Sold to Interglobal Shipping 3001 Ltd.,
Tel Aviv, Israel and renamed GB EUROPE.
2.2014: Still listed by 'Lloyd's Register'

Robrix (5) was part of the fleet for less than two years. *[FotoFlite incorporating Skyfotos, 285630]*

55. LIZRIX (2) 2008- Chemical/products tanker
IMO 9428188 1,343g 600n 1,942d
76.47 x 10.60 x 4.420 metres
4SCSA 6-cyl. oil engine by Yanmar Diesel

Engine Co. Ltd., Amagasaki, Japan; 1,300 BHP, 11 knots.
17.12.2007: Launched by Selahattin Telci Gemi Yapim Sanayi ve Ticaret Ltd. Sti, Turkey (Yard No. 102) for The Lizrix

Tankship Ltd. (Rix Shipping Co. Ltd., managers), Hull as LIZRIX.
27.5.2008: Completed.
3.2011: Registered in the Isle of Man.
2.2014: In the current fleet.

Lizrix (2). [FotoFlite incorporating Skyfotos, 332028]

56. LERRIX (2) 2012- Oil products tanker
IMO 9599377 801g 340n 1,316d
53.0 x 10.0 x 4.0 metres
Two 4SCSA 6-cyl. oil engines by Cummins

Engine Co. Inc., U.S.A.; 608 BHP, 9 knots.
22.4.2012: Launched by Hepworth Shipyard Ltd., Paull (Yard No.166) for Rix Shipping Co. Ltd., Hull as LERRIX and registered in the Isle of Man.

The forward part of the hull was built by Aveco (Teeside) Ltd., Middlesbrough.
7.9.2012: Completed.
2.2014: In current fleet.

Lerrix (2) during her naming by Lucinda Emily Rix in the William Wright Dock, Hull. She is essentially a sea-going bunkering tanker, with the ability to blend bunkering products on board. *[Company archives]*

Lerrix (2) sailing from Alexandra Dock on 10th November 2012. *[Roy Cressey]*

Estuarial tank barges

1. BELDALE H/RIX OSPREY 1976-2008 Black oil tank barge

O.N. 301620 IMO 7938969 207g 129n
50.91 x 5.19 x 2.286 metres
4SCSA 8-cyl. oil engine by L. Gardner and Sons Ltd., Manchester; 152 BHP. Later replaced by an oil engine by the Caterpillar Tractor Co., Peoria, Illinois, USA.

1.9.1959: Launched by John Harker (Shipyards) Ltd., Knottingley (Yard No. 284) for John Harker Ltd., Knottingley as BELDALE H.
1959: Completed.
1976: Acquired by J.R. Rix and Sons Ltd., Hull.
1978: Transferred to T. and S. Rix Ltd., Hull.
1979: Rebuilt.
1987: Managers became Rix Shipping Co. Ltd., Hull.
1996: Renamed RIX OSPREY.
1999: Transferred to The Rix Osprey Shipping Co. Ltd. (Rix Shipping Co. Ltd., managers), Hull.
2003: Transferred to T. and S. Rix Ltd. (Rix Shipping Co. Ltd., managers), Hull.
2004: Transferred to The Rix Osprey Tankship Ltd. (Rix Shipping Co. Ltd., managers), Hull.
2006: Laid up at Hull and stripped of all useful parts.
2008: Sold to Alan G. Pease, Goole and offered for resale and conversion to a house boat.

2. BURDALE H/RIX KESTREL 1976–2008 Tank barge

O.N. 186753 206g 119n 320d
50.91 x 5.36 x 2.286 metres
4SCSA 8-cyl. oil engine by L. Gardner and Sons Ltd., Manchester; 152 BHP.
7.2.1957: Launched by John Harker (Shipyards) Ltd., Knottingley (Yard No. 278) for John Harker Ltd., Knottingley as BURDALE H.
1957: Completed.
1976: Acquired by J.R. Rix and Sons Ltd., Hull.
1978: Transferred to T. and S. Rix Ltd., Hull.
1987: Managers became Rix Shipping Co. Ltd., Hull.
1993: Renamed RIX KESTREL.
1999: Transferred to The Rix Kestrel Shipping Co. Ltd. (Rix Shipping Co. Ltd., managers), Hull.
2003: Transferred to T. and S. Rix Ltd. (Rix Shipping Co. Ltd., managers), Hull.
2004: Transferred to The Rix Kestrel Tankship Ltd. (Rix Shipping Co. Ltd., managers), Hull.
2006: Laid up at Hull and stripped of all useful parts.
2008: Sold for demolition.

Above: *Rix Osprey* at Grimsby before rebuilding. *[Roy Cressey]*

Below: *Rix Osprey* after rebuilding. *[Roy Cressey]*

Rix Kestrel about to leave Ocean Lock, Goole. *[Company archives]*

3. BURTONDALE H/RIX FALCON/RIX PHOENIX 1976-
Clean oil tank barge

O.N. 301639 IMO 9392638
172g 102n 250d
43.29 x 5.41 x 2.134 metres
2007: 365g 165n 500d
59.01 x 6.08 x 2.22 metres
4SCSA 8-cyl. oil engine by
L. Gardner and Sons Ltd.,
Manchester; 152 BHP.
2007: 4SCSA 6-cyl. oil engine by
Caterpillar Inc., Peoria, Illinois,
USA; 475 BHP.
3.5.1960: Launched by John
Harker (Shipyards) Ltd.,
Knottingley (Yard No. 289) for
John Harker Ltd., Knottingley as
BURTONDALE H.
1960: Completed.
1976: Acquired by J.R. Rix and
Sons Ltd., Hull.
1978: Transferred to T. and S. Rix
Ltd., Hull.
1987: Managers became Rix
Shipping Co. Ltd., Hull.
1992: Renamed RIX FALCON.
1999: Transferred to The Rix
Falcon Shipping Co. Ltd. (Rix
Shipping Co. Ltd., managers), Hull.
2001: New midships tank section
fitted by Hepworth Shipyard Ltd.,
Paull.
2003: Transferred to T and S.
Rix Ltd. (Rix Shipping Co. Ltd.,
managers), Hull.
2004: Transferred to The Rix
Falcon Tankship Ltd. (Rix
Shipping Co. Ltd., managers),
Hull.
1.2007: New bow, stern and cargo
section fitted at Hepworth Shipyard
Ltd., Paull, owners became The
Rix Phoenix Tankship Ltd. (Rix
Shipping Co. Ltd., managers), Hull
and renamed RIX PHOENIX.
2009: Double hull fitted around
her cargo section by Aveco Ltd.,
Middlesbrough.
2.2014: In the current fleet.

Top: *Rix Falcon* in original
condition leaving the BSC Jetty,
Immingham after delivering
bunkers. *[Company archives]*

Middle: Now renamed, *Rix
Phoenix* approaching Ballholme
Lock, Castleford after being
lengthened and fitted with a
new bow, cargo section and
stern. *[Company archives]*

Bottom: In the Tees on 17th
January 2010 after having a
second skin fitted to make her a
double skinned tanker. Anchors
have also been fitted. *[Michael
Green]*

4. RIX EAGLE 1990- Clean oil tank barge
O.N. 709235 316g 207n
55.95 x 6.0 x 2.98 metres
4SCSA 6-cyl. oil engine by Caterpillar Tractor Co., Peoria, Illinois, USA; 475 BHP.
3.4.1990: Completed by Hepworth Shipyard Ltd., Paull (Yard No. 137) for The Rix Eagle Shipping Co. Ltd. (Rix Shipping Co. Ltd., managers), Hull as RIX EAGLE.
1995: Lengthened by Hepworth Shipyard Ltd., Paull.
2003: Transferred to T. and S. Rix Ltd. (Rix Shipping Co. Ltd., managers), Hull.
2003: Transferred to The Rix Eagle Tankship Co. Ltd. (Rix Shipping Co. Ltd., managers), Hull.
2.2014: In the current fleet.

5. ARTEMISIUM/RIX MERLIN (1) 1996-2003 Clean oil tank barge
IMO 8036718 299g 500d
53.83 x 7.1 x 2.6 metres
Oil engine by Bolnes; 300 BHP.
9.1985: 4SCSA 8-cyl. oil engine by Caterpillar Tractor Co., Peoria, Illinois, USA; 449 BHP.
1964: Completed by N.V. Scheepswerven 'Piet Hein' v/h Firma W. Schram & Zonen, Bolnes/Papendrecht, Netherlands (Yard No. 709) for Maatschappij Bendelaer, Krimpen a/d Lek, Netherlands as ARTEMISIUM.
c.1980: Sold to C. Crawley and Sons Ltd., London.
1996: Acquired by T. and S. Rix Ltd.. (Rix Shipping Co. Ltd., managers), Hull.
1998: Renamed RIX MERLIN.
1.1.2001: Transferred to Rix Merlin Shipping Co. Ltd. (Rix Shipping Co. Ltd., managers), Hull.
3.3.2003: Transferred to Rix Tankships Ltd. (Rix Shipping Co. Ltd., managers), Hull.
2.4.2003: Transferred to The Rix Merlin Tankship Ltd. (Rix Shipping Co. Ltd., managers), Hull.
11.7.2003: Sold for demolition after being stripped of useful parts and broken up on the Humber at New Holland.

Top: Rix Eagle being lengthened by Hepworth Shipyard Ltd. *[Company archives]*
Above: Good luck or good management? *Rix Eagle passes* under the bridge just as a Total Butler road tanker, for whom oil was transported, happens to be crossing. *[Company archives]*

Rix Merlin (1) at Hull. The accommodation confirms her Dutch origin. *[Roy Cressey]*

6. RIX OWL 2003- Clean oil short-sea tank barge
IMO 9283588 316g 207n 500d
60.8 x 6.1 x 2.4 metres
4SCSA 6-cyl. oil engine by
Caterpillar Tractor Co., Peoria,
Illinois, USA; 405 BHP.
1.2003: Completed by Hepworth
Shipyard Ltd., Paull (Yard No.
158) for The Rix Owl Tankship
Ltd. (Rix Shipping Co. Ltd.,
managers), Hull as RIX OWL.
3.3.2010: Arrived in tow on
the Tees to be rebuilt with a
double hull by Aveco Ltd.,
Middlesbrough.
2.2014: In the current fleet.

**7. RIX MERLIN (2) 2006-
Clean oil tank barge**
O.N. 910768 IMO 9366952
496g 205n
52.8 x 7.9 x 2.6 metres
4SCSA 6-cyl. oil engine by
Cummins Engine Co. Ltd.,
Daventry; 653 BHP.
17.9.2005: Launched by
Hepworth Shipyard, Paull (Yard
No. 159) for The Rix Merlin
Tankship Ltd. (Rix Shipping Co.
Ltd., managers), Hull as RIX
MERLIN.
1.11.2005: Completed.
2008: Transferred to J.R. Rix and
Sons Ltd., Hull.
2.2014: In the current fleet.

Rix Owl (top) on the slipway at
Paull. *[Company archives]*
The double-skinned tanker
Rix Merlin (2) on the Humber
(middle) and on 14th July 2008
(bottom) *[Company archives;
Michael Green]*.

RIX PANTHER 2012- Aluminium wind farm service vessel
18.9 x 7.2 x 1.4 metres.
Two Cummins QSK19 diesel engines driving twin screws; each 800 BHP, 29 knots.
20.7.2012: Delivered by Alnmaritec Ltd., Blyth (Yard No. ALN 145) for Rix Sea Shuttle Ltd., Hull as RIX PANTHER.
2.2014: In current fleet.

RIX TIGER 2013- Aluminium wind farm service vessel
18.9 x 7.2 x 1.4 metres.
Two Cummins QSK19 diesel engines driving twin screws; each 800 BHP, 29 knots.
29.7.2013: Delivered by Alnmaritec Ltd., Blyth (Yard No. ALN 156) for Rix Sea Shuttle Ltd., Hull as RIX TIGER.
2.2014: In current fleet.

RIX CHEETAH 2013- Aluminium wind farm service vessel
21.3 x 6.4 x 1.7 metres.
Two CAT C32 diesel engines driving twin screws; each 1,320 BHP, 29 knots.
22.8.2013: Delivered by Dunston Shipbuilders from Hepworth Shipyard Ltd., Paull for Rix Sea Shuttle Ltd., Hull as RIX CHEETAH.
2.2014: In current fleet.

Aluminium wind farm service vessels *Rix Panther* (right) and *Rix Tiger* have a crew of two or three, seats for 12 passengers, a five-tonnes payload and a speed of 24 knots. *[Company archives]*

Completed by Dunston Shipbuilders at Hepworth Shipyard, Paull, *Rix Cheetah* is a larger design of workboat, capable of 29 knots. Further vessels of this type are on order from the Hepworth Shipyard. *[Company archives]*

John Robert Rix, Hull

HOLMAN SUTCLIFFE 1913 Iron
O.N. 60309 203g 76n
123.3 x 19.6 x 9.8 feet
1906: 130.5 feet
C. 2-cyl. by the Greenock Foundry Co.,
Greenock.
1878: C. 2-cyl. by R. Smith, Preston.
12.1867: Launched by Swan Brothers,
Maryhill, Dumbarton for Hugh Andrews,
Belfast as LADY ALICE KENLIS.
1871: Sold to Edward Henesey and Co.,
Dundrum.
1874: Sold to John Paley, Preston.
1878: Sold to John Jackson and Co., Preston.
1887: Sold to Thomas Jackson, Preston.
1890: Sold to Edward R. Jones, Liverpool.
1895: Transferred to Mrs. Louisa Jones
(Edward R. Jones, manager), Liverpool.
2.12.1908: Sold to Sutcliffe and Co., Boston.
6.1.1909: Renamed HOLMAN
SUTCLIFFE.
25.3.1913: Sold to John R. Rix, Hull.
13.11.1913: Sold to George F. Peters, Bristol.
2.1.1916: Transferred to Mrs. Mary J. Peters.
7.4.1924: Transferred to the Bristol Sand
and Gravel Co. Ltd. (Frederick E. Peters,
manager), Bristol.
20.6.1930: Sold to Stewart Pollock,
Wivenhoe for breaking up.
She is also reported to have been broken up
by John Cashmore, Newport.

Managed on behalf of other owners by Robert Rix and J.R. Rix and Sons Ltd.

1. WALSTREAM 1964
O.N. 187386 485g 242n 625d
167.5 x 27.1 x 10.8 feet
2SCSA 6-cyl. oil engine by N.V. Boele's
Scheepswerven en Machinefabriek, Bolnes,
Netherlands; 450 BHP.
1949: Completed by G.J. Van der
Werf's Scheepsbouw N.V., Westerbroek,
Netherlands (Yard No. 256) for O/Y Suomi
Shipping A/B (C.S. Bergstrom, manager),
Helsingfors, Finland as ZENITA.
1950: Managers became A/B R. Nordstrom
and Co. O/Y, Lovisa, Finland and renamed
KAARINA.
1950: Sold to Basse and Co., Copenhagen,
Denmark and renamed JORGEN BASS.
1956: Sold to Walford Line Ltd., London
and renamed WALSTREAM.
1964: Managers became J.R. Rix and Sons
Ltd., Hull.
1964: Sold Avlis Shipping Co. Special S.A.
(G. Dracopoulos and B. Athanassiades),
Piraeus, Greece and renamed AVLIS.
1969: Sold to Prodomos Shipping Co. S.A.,
Piraeus, Greece and renamed LARYMNA.
1974: Sold to Demimar Shipping Co.
S.A. (Phoebus D. Kyprianou, manager),
Limassol, Cyprus and renamed PATRICK.
1983: Reported broken up at Piraeus
following fire damage sustained in 1978.

Holman Sutcliffe. [J. and M. Clarkson collection]

Walstream. [World Ship Society Ltd.]

Managed on behalf of the Ministry of Shipping and Ministry of War Transport, later Ministry of Transport, London by Robert Rix and Sons

2. H.H. PETERSEN 1940-1941
O.N. 167444 975n 570n
221.7 x 35.0 x 12.8 feet
T.3-cyl. by Flensburger Schiffsbau-
Gesellschaft, Flensburg, Germany; 105 NHP.
1927: Completed by H.C. Christensens
Staalskibsvaerft A/S, Marstal, Denmark
(Yard No. 42) for D/S A/S 'Emmanuel'
(Alfr. Petersen, manager), Marstal, Denmark
as H.H. PETERSEN.

9.4.1940: Requisitioned by The United Kingdom.
7.5.1940: Registered in the ownership of the
Ministry of Shipping, London (Robert Rix
and Sons, Hull, managers).
7.1.1941: Mined and sunk in position 52.22
north, 02.05 east whilst on a voyage from
Goole to Rochester with a cargo of coal.
27.2.1941: Register closed.

3. EMPIRE FORD 1941-1943
O.N.167108 320g 150n
131.5 x 24.5 x 8.8 feet
2SCSA 6-cyl. oil engine by H. Widdop and
Co. Ltd., Keighley; 375 BHP, 9 knots.
1951: 4SCSA 6-cyl. oil engine by Société
Generale de Constructions Mecanique, La
Courneuve, France.
28.5.1941: Launched by J.S. Watson
(Gainsborough) Ltd., Gainsborough (Yard
No. 1520).

17.9.1941: Registered in the ownership of the Ministry of War Transport, London (Robert Rix and Sons, Hull, managers) as EMPIRE FORD.
10.1.1943: Grounded and engine room flooded off Seahouses, North Sunderland.
11.1.1943: Abandoned with her cement cargo in a sinking condition. Refloated and anchored but later broke adrift in heavy weather and grounded off the Farne Islands near Bamburgh, Northumberland.
27.2.1943: Refloated and towed into Amble.
6.3.1943: Arrived in the Tyne under tow for repairs.
7.9.1943: Register closed on transfer to The Royal Netherlands Government (Netherlands Ministry of Shipping and Fisheries, managers), London and renamed NOORDERHAVEN.
1947: Sold to Société de Caboteurs Reunis (L.J. Giraud, manager), Cannes, France and renamed SAINT HONORAT.
1950: Sold to Société Navale d'Import et d'Export, Bordeaux, later Société Navale d'Importation et d'Exportation, Paris, France.
1951: Re-engined.
1965: Sold to D. Vassilatos (Kontos and Son, managers), Piraeus, Greece and renamed KORALI.
1966: Sold to K. Savva Brothers (Spyridon Athanasoulias, managers), Piraeus and renamed MARIA S.
1967: Sold to P. and M. Gogis and K. Michaels, Piraeus and renamed SOFIA GOGI.
1975: Sold to Greek owners and renamed KONSTANTINOS GAVIOTIS.
1976: Sold to Georgios Atsalis and Co., Piraeus and renamed AGIOS GEORGIS.
1992: Deleted from 'Lloyd's Register' as continued existence in doubt.

4. EMPIRE SPORTSMAN 1943-1946
See NORRIX (4) in Robert Rix and Sons fleet list

5. EMPIRE FAVOURITE 1944-1946
O.N. 180120 410g 189n 450d
142.2 x 27.0 x 8.5 feet
4SCSA 7-cyl. oil engine by Blackstone and Co. Ltd., Stamford.
1950: 2SCSA 6-cyl. oil engine by Newbury Diesel Co. Ltd., Newbury.
10.7.1944: Launched by Goole Shipbuilding and Repairing Co. Ltd., Goole (Yard No. 419) for the Ministry of War Transport, London (Robert Rix and Sons, Hull, managers) as EMPIRE FAVOURITE.
7.1944: Completed.
4.1946: Transferred to The Ministry of Transport, London.
8.1946: Sold to F.T. Everard and Sons Ltd., Greenhithe and renamed FORMALITY.
1950: Re-engined.
1961: Laid up awaiting disposal.
3.1962: Sold to T.W. Ward Ltd., Grays.
8.1962: Resold to Metaal Handel & Sloopwerken H.P. Heulvelman for breaking

Empire Fabric was managed by Robert Rix and Sons for a little under two years. *[World Ship Society Ltd.]*

Robert Rix and Sons managed the *Empire Favourite*, later Everard's *Formality* (above) from completion at Goole in July 1944 until August 1946. *[J. and M. Clarkson]*

up at Krimpen-aan-den-Ijssel, Netherlands.
13.8.1962: Demolition began.

6. EMPIRE FABRIC 1944-1946
O.N.180277 411g 178n 400d
142.2 x 27.0 x 8.5 feet
4SCSA 5-cyl. oil engine by Ruston and Hornsby Ltd., Lincoln.
1944: Laid down as CHANT 14 and while under construction renamed FABRIC 14.
6.1944: Completed by Henry Scarr Ltd., Hessle (Yard No. 447) for the Ministry of War Transport, London (Robert Rix and Sons, Hull, managers) as EMPIRE FABRIC.
4.1946: Transferred to the Ministry of Transport, London (G.F. Cuthbert Brown and Co. Ltd., Newcastle-upon-Tyne, managers).
1948: Managers became Bauer and Co., London.
1949: Sold to Harbour Specialities Ltd. (Phillip Bauer, manager), London.
1950: Sold to Fenstock Shipping Co. Ltd. (Cecil J. Orchard, manager), London and renamed FENSTOCK.

1952: Sold to Torridge Coasters Ltd., Appledore and renamed TORRIDGE LASS.
1964: Sold to E. Desgagne, Quebec, Canada and renamed STE. MARGUERITE.
1966: Sold to Citadelle Navigation Inc., Quebec.
1966: Sold to Bouchard Navigation Ltée. (Euclide Bouchard, managers), Quebec.
1970: Sold to N. Harvey, Ile aux Coudres, Quebec.
1972: Renamed PRINCE LOYS.
1975: Sold to F. Lussier, Canada and later scrapped at Ile-aux-Coudres, Canada, having been laid up with engine trouble since 10.1972.

7. EMPIRE CONLEA 1945-1947
O.N. 180984 216g 155n
129.4 x 23.0 x 8.0 feet.
4SCSA 4-cyl. oil engine by Deutsche Werk Kiel A.G., Kiel, Germany, fitted in 1942.
1939: Completed by Werft Nobiskrug Schiffbau G.m.b.H., Rendsburg, Germany (Yard No.261) for German owners as GUNTHER HARTMANN.

5.1945: Seized by Allied forces at Heligoland, allocated to the Ministry of War Transport, London (Robert Rix and Sons, Hull, managers) and renamed EMPIRE CONLEA.

1946: Transferred to the Ministry of Transport, London (R. Rix and Sons, Hull, managers).

1947: Sold to Jeppesen Heaton Ltd., London.

1950: Renamed CONLEA.

10.2.1956: Foundered in heavy weather after her fore hatch was stove in while on a voyage from Eling, near Southampton, to St. Malo with a cargo of pitch. She sank 15 miles south west of the Corbiere Light, Jersey with the loss of one crew member.

Conlea. [World Ship Society Ltd.]

Hepworth Shipyard Ltd.

John R. Hepworth and his son began repairing small vessels in Queen's Dock, Hull in 1926, moving in 1930 to premises on the River Hull. In 1933, as John R. Hepworth and Co. (Hull) Ltd., they moved to the present site at Paull, on the north bank of the Humber about two miles downstream of Hull. The yard began building vessels in 1947, with four barges for Brazil, and a dry dock 130 by 20 feet was added the next year, and a slipway in 1957.

The yard's output included motor barges, lighters, tugs, pontoons and fishing vessels, with a sprinkling of coasters. First of the coasters is believed to have been the *Abbots Leigh* (1955/147) for F.A. Ashmead and Son Ltd. of Bristol, whilst *Paullgate* (1961/200) for Hull Gates Shipping Co. Ltd. was aptly named. A major customer was the London and Rochester Trading Co. Ltd. with *Ignition*

(1967/199), *Jubilation* (1967/199) and *Blatence* (1969/392) plus the motor barges *Rogul* (1965/172), *Roina* (1966/172), *Locator* 1970/191) and *Lodella* (1970/196). The yard closed in 1973, having built 121 craft and having slipped or dry docked a massive total of 1,034 vessels.

J.R. Rix and Sons Ltd. took over the derelict yard in 1977, and rebuilt and re-equipped it, forming a new subsidiary, Hepworth Shipyard Ltd. The yard numbering sequence was continued, prefixed RIX, with the vessels listed below being completed, mainly fishing craft and tugs plus tank barges for their own account. Maintenance, repair and rebuilding work has continued, partly for Rix's own fleet with *Rix Harrier* and *Rix Hawk* being converted from dry cargo to tank barges. Recently, management of the workforce has been entrusted to Dunston Shipbuilders.

Yard No	Name	Date	GRT	Type	Owner
	Yard numbers from this point prefixed by RIX				
122	*St. Leger*	1978	120	Fishing	Jack Robinson (Hull) Ltd., Hull
123	*St. Apollo*	1978	120	Fishing	Jack Robinson (Hull) Ltd., Hull
124	*St. Kilda*	1978	120	Fishing	Jack Robinson (Hull) Ltd., Hull
125	*Sharrona*	1980	120	Fishing	
126	-	1981		Light float	Middle Whitton Light Float
127	*Bandit*	1982		Water taxi	J.R. Rix and Sons Ltd., Hull
128	*Ross Argos*	1983	104	Fishing	
129	*Aztec*	1986	116	Fishing	George A. Finlay, Kirkcudbright
130	*Pentland Venture*	1986	186	Ferry	I. Thomas, Aberdeen
131	*Horizon II*	1987	125	Fishing	James Reid, Fraserburgh
132	*Q Varl*	1988	86	Fishing	Michael J.W. Hall and others, Ballantrae
133	*Sardonyx I*	1988	134	Fishing	Peter and J. Johnstone Ltd., Aberdeen
134	*Aquila*	1988	120	Fishing	George A. Finlay, Kirkcudbright
135	*Kookaburra*	1989	105	Fishing	
136	*Nichtola*	1989	93	Cockle dredger	J. Robinson (Trawlers) Ltd., Ballantrae
137	*Rix Eagle*	1990	292	Tank barge	J.R. Rix and Sons Ltd., Hull
138	*Tobrach-N*	1991	160	Trawler	M.J.W. Hall and T.I. Nicholson, Troon

Barge sections in the yard at Paull. *[Company archives]*

139	*Atlantis Bell*	1989	125	Cockle dredger	Halcombe Merchants Ltd., Newry
140	*Azula*	1990	114	Fishing	George A. Finlay, Kirkcudbright
141	*Aquinus*	1992	128	Fishing	George A. Finlay, Kirkcudbright
142	*Solway Harvester*	1992	146	Fishing	J. Robinson (Trawlers) Ltd., Ballintrae
143	*Sardonyx II*	1993	119	Fishing	Peter and J. Johnstone Ltd., Aberdeen
144	*Wyeforce*	1994	57	Tug	Itchen Marine Towage Ltd., Southampton
-	*Rebecca M.*	1994	322	Work boat	Humber Workboats (Barton) Ltd.
	The above is a re-construction of a US Army barge Job No 2083/6				
145	*Askari*	1994	17	Cockle dredger	George A. Finlay, Kirkcudbright
146	*Nosterfield*	1995		Dredger	
147	*Argosy*	1996	110	Fishing	G.A. Finlay and A. Keer, Ballantrae
148	*Afon Goch*	1997	123	Tug	Holyhead Towing Co. Ltd., Beaumaris
149	*Jubilee Quest*	1997	178	Fishing	Olbek Fishing Co. Ltd., Grimsby
150	*Kingfisher*	1998	163	Fishing	West Coast Sea Products Ltd., Ballantrae
151	*Academus*	1998	35		
152	*Solway Ranger*	1999	146	Fishing	J. Robinson (Trawlers) Ltd., Ballintrae

Work in progress at Hepworth Shipyard.
Middle; *Rix Harrier* slipped at Paull in October 1996 during her conversion from dry cargo vessel to bunkering tanker.
Bottom; *Breydon Venture/Rix Hawk* (left/right) undergoing a similar conversion in 1999. *[All Michael Green]*

-	*Rix Falcon*	2000		New tank section	J.R. Rix and Sons Ltd., Hull
153	*Fairline*	2000	168	Fishing	Caley Fisheries Ltd., Peterhead
154	*King Explorer*	2001	159	Fishing	
155	*St. Oswald*	2001		FPV	
156	*Afon Cefni*	2002	140	Tug	Holyhead Towing Co. Ltd., Beaumaris
157	*Afon Alaw*	2002	200	Tug	Holyhead Towing Co. Ltd., Beaumaris
158	*Rix Owl*	2003	320	Tank barge	J.R. Rix and Sons Ltd., Hull
159	*Rix Merlin* (2)	2005	496	Tanker	J.R. Rix and Sons Ltd., Hull

Rix Merlin under construction in the Hepworth Shipyard on 28th May 2005. *[Michael Green]*

The lengthened *Rix Phoenix* passing Whitgift on the Ouse. She was later fitted with a second skin around her cargo section to make her a double-hulled tank barge. *[Company archives]*

160	*Afon Braint*	2005	147	Tug	Holyhead Towing Co. Ltd., Beaumaris
161	*1.2007*: New bow, stern and cargo section fitted to *Rix Falcon*, vessel renamed *Rix Phoenix*.				
162	*Afon Caradog*	2007		Tug	Holyhead Towing Co. Ltd., Beaumaris
163	-	2007	473	Tug	Holyhead Towing Co. Ltd., Beaumaris
164	*Lerrix* (2)	2012	1,200	Tanker	J.R. Rix and Sons Ltd., Hull
	Rix Cheetah	2013		Work boat	J.R. Rix and Sons Ltd., Hull
The brief history of the yard is taken from an article by Mike Taylor in the journal 'Archive' No. 59, published in September 2008, and which includes some excellent pictures of the motor barges. Many thanks to Captain John Landels of the WSS Yard List Team for the details above.					

The hull of *Ak Bars* (above) was constructed by Aveco at Middlesbrough and brought to Paull to be fitted out by the Hepworth Shipyard. The tug had been designed by her owners the Holyhead Towing Co.Ltd. and was completed in June 2009 for service in the Caspian Sea. Soon after delivery *Ak Bars* was put under the Cypriot flag and renamed *Al Burkut*. *(Michael Green)*

INDEX OF SHIPS
All vessels mentioned are listed, including proposed names and names of cancelled vessels, with dates of completion if known.

Magrix (2) (1938) 16-17,19-23,26,29,65,67

Magrix (3) (1976) 37,39-40,76

Majo (1965) 32,72

Malrix (1923) 8-10,12,18,62

Maltese Venture (1972) 74

Maraboe (1931) 67

Maria S (1941) 91

Marine Duval (1944) 74

Mayrix (1920) 8,10,12,17,59-60

Moorside (1921) 9,62

Nan 1 (1957) 71

Nautica (1963) 70

Nautica (1968) 33

Nellie M (1972) 36,74

Nettuno (1937) 64

Neukloster (1977) 82

Neuwulmstorf (1977) 82

Ngarua (1931) 67

Nichtola (1989) 92

Nicky L (1976) 76

Noorderhaven (1941) 91

Noorderhaven (1951) 28

Noord-Holland (tug) 35

Norbritt (1917) 14,17-8,63

Nordholm (1976) 79

Nordic Bridge (1991) 82

Normandy Coast (1916) 18,65

Norrix (1) (1920) 7-8,59-60

Norrix (2) (1914) 8,10,61-2,96

Norrix (3) (1930) 12,14-5,19,63-4

Norrix (4) (1943) 19-20,67,91

Northgate (1964) 33

Nosterfield (1995) 93

Oarsman (1958) 39

Oceanic Lady (1972) 75

Okiki (1967) 82

Orkney Dawn (1916) 58

Orselina (1938) 66

Owain Tudur (1883) 6,55-6

Owenro (1965) 33,73

Paola X (1947) 67

Patrick (1949) 90

Paullgate (1961) 92

Peggy Grieve (1883) 56

Pegrix (1) (1921) 9,12-3,17,62-3

Pegrix (2) (1938) 17-18,23,65

Pentland Venture (1986) 92

Pert (1892) 1,5-7,54-5

Plover (1892) 55

Plympton (1930) 64

Pointsman (1934) 7

Polgarth (1920) 60

Polkerris (1921) 60

Poolena (1892) 55

Port Renard (1961) 35

Prince Loys (1944) 91

Princess 4

Pursuit (1937) 64

Q Varl (1988) 92

Quickthorn (1908) 56

R & M (1881) 4-6,54

Rebecca M. (1994) 93

Restorer II (1977) 78

Rix Cheetah (2013) 1,50-1,89,94

Rix Condor (1967) 42,44-5,81

Rix Eagle (1990) 42,44-5,87,92

Rix Falcon (1960) 41,44,86,94

Rix Harrier (1979) 42-5,78,93

Rix Hawk (1977) 42,44-5,78,93

Rix Kestrel (1957) 41,44-5,85

Rix Merlin (1) (1964) 43,87

Rix Merlin (2) (2005) 42-5,88,94

Rix Osprey (1959) 41-2,44-5,85

Rix Owl (2003) 42-5,88,94

Rix Panther (2012) 50-1,89

Rix Phoenix (1960) 42-3,45,86,94

Rix Tiger (2013) 50,89

Robrix (1) (1916) 6,12,58

Robrix (2) (1917) 12,14,20,63

Robrix (3) (1937) 1, 14-15,17-20,23,36,64

Robrix (4) (1974) 34,37,39,48,75

Robrix (5) (1991) 50,82-3

Roelof Holwerda (1976) 76

Rogul (1965) 92

Roina (1966) 92

Ronrix (1977) 48,50,82

Ross Argos (1983) 92

Roxton (1931) 21,67-8

Saint Honorat (1941) 91

Salrix (1) (1965) 31,33,36-7,39,73

Salrix (2) (1977) 33,48,50,82

Sanderskopel (1977) 80

Sardonyx I (1988) 92

Sardonyx II (1993) 93

Saxon Queen (1904) 6,56,57

Schwalbe (1898) 6,54

Seaman (1985, tug) 76

Seebär (1941) 30

Shaman 1 (1957) 71

Sharrona (1980) 92

Siggen (1977) 80

Siggen II (1977) 80

Silja (1967) 81

Silloth Stag (1974) 36-7,75

Sofia Gogi (1941) 91

Solway Harvester (1992) 93

Solway Ranger (1999) 93

Speedwell (1917) (proposed) 63

Spezi (1972) 74

Springouse (1917) 59

Sprite (1974) 76

Spurnpoint (1908) 6-7,56

St. Apollo (1978) 92

St. Kilda (1978) 92

St. Leger (1978) 92

St. Oswald (2001) 94

Ste. Marguerite (1944) 91

Stefan (1977) 80

Taffy (1894) 6,57

Tanja Holwerda (1976) 76

Teos (1977) 81

Tern (1932) 14-15

The Dutch (1976) 37,76

Tilstone Maid (1974) 75

Timrix (1) (1965) 31-2,72

Timrix (2) (1972) 34,36-7,48,74-5

Timrix (3) (1977) 48,50,80-1

Timrix (4) (cancelled) 44

Tobrach-N (1991) 92

Torridge Lass (1944) 91

Torwood (1930) 64

Towing Chieftan (1963, tug) 71

Turquoise (1947) 67

Ulla (1991) 82

Union Crystal (1965) 73

Urouba 1 (1957) 71

Utrecht (tug) 30

Wael II (1965) 73

Walstream (1949) 28,90

Wansbeck 32

Warren Court (1917) 63

Warrenpoint (1892) 5-6,54

Werfen (1991) 82

Whitehaven (1957) 29,71

Whitgift (1917) 12,63

World Champion (1969) 35

Wyeforce (1994) 93

Yokefleet (1910) 9

Yorksee (1977) 48,79

Young Ann (1937) 64

Zenita (1949) 90

A naive painting of *Norrix* (2), possibly at Berwick-on-Tweed.
[Couresy Gwen Lancaster, great great grand daughter of the artist]